GREAT
LIBRARY EVENTS

MEDICAL LIBRARY ASSOCIATION BOOKS

The Medical Library Association (MLA) publishes state-of-the-art books that enhance health care, support professional development, improve library services, and promote research throughout the world.

MLA books are dynamic resources for librarians in hospitals, medical research practice, corporate libraries, and other settings. These invaluable publications provide medical librarians, health care professionals, and patients with accurate information that can improve outcomes and save lives.

The MLA Books Panel is responsible for (1) monitoring publishing trends within the industry; (2) exploring new concepts in publications by actively soliciting and proposing ideas for new publications; and (3) coordinating publishing efforts to achieve the best utilization of MLA resources. Each MLA book is directly administered from its inception by the MLA Books Panel, composed of MLA members with expertise spanning the breadth of health sciences librarianship.

MEDICAL LIBRARY ASSOCIATION BOOKS PANEL

Carolann Curry, Chair
Jamie L. Conklin
Rebecca Harrington, AHIP
Claire B. Joseph, AHIP
Ivan Portillo, AHIP
Vedana Vaidhyanathan
Erin Watson, AHIP
Beverly Murphy, AHIP, FMLA, Board Liaison

ABOUT THE MEDICAL LIBRARY ASSOCIATION

The Medical Library Association (MLA) is a global, nonprofit educational organization, with a membership of more than 400 institutions and 3,000 professionals in the health information field. Since 1898, MLA has fostered excellence in the professional practice and leadership of health sciences library and information professionals to enhance health care, education, and research throughout the world. MLA educates health information professionals, supports health information research, promotes access to the world's health sciences information, and works to ensure that the best health information is available to all.

RECENTLY PUBLISHED MLA BOOKS

3D Printing in Medical Libraries: A Crash Course in Supporting Innovation in Healthcare by Jennifer Herron

Diversity and Inclusion in Libraries: A Call to Action and Strategies for Success edited by Shannon D. Jones and Beverly Murphy

Framing Health Care Instruction: An Information Literacy Handbook for the Health Sciences by Lauren M. Young and Elizabeth G. Hinton

The Clinical Medical Librarian's Handbook edited by Judy C. Stribling

The Engaged Health Sciences Library Liaison edited by Lindsay Alcock and Kelly Thormodson

A History of Medical Libraries and Medical Librarianship: From John Shaw Billings to the Digital Era by Michael R. Kronenfeld and Jennie Jacobs Kronenfeld

Planning and Promoting Events in Health Sciences Libraries: Success Stories and Best Practices edited by Shalu Gillum and Natasha Williams

Great Library Events: From Planning to Promotion to Evaluation by Mary Grace Flaherty

GREAT LIBRARY EVENTS

From Planning to Promotion to Evaluation

Mary Grace Flaherty

ROWMAN & LITTLEFIELD
Lanham • Boulder • New York • London

Published by Rowman & Littlefield
An imprint of The Rowman & Littlefield Publishing Group, Inc.
4501 Forbes Boulevard, Suite 200, Lanham, Maryland 20706
www.rowman.com

6 Tinworth Street, London, SE11 5AL, United Kingdom

Copyright © 2021 by Medical Library Association

All rights reserved. No part of this book may be reproduced in any form or by any electronic or mechanical means, including information storage and retrieval systems, without written permission from the publisher, except by a reviewer who may quote passages in a review.

British Library Cataloguing in Publication Information Available

Library of Congress Cataloging-in-Publication Data

Names: Flaherty, Mary Grace, 1960– author.
Title: Great library events : from planning to promotion to evaluation / Mary Grace Flaherty.
Description: Lanham : Rowman & Littlefield, [2021] | Series: Medical Library Association books | Includes bibliographical references and index. | Summary: "Here is an accessible guidebook for hosting successful library events. From the first steps of defining the scope of an event to finding funding, to marketing and publicizing, evaluating, reporting and using data to keep the program cycle going, this guide is full of practical examples and tools"— Provided by publisher.
Identifiers: LCCN 2020052316 (print) | LCCN 2020052317 (ebook) | ISBN 9781538137048 (cloth) | ISBN 9781538137055 (paperback) | ISBN 9781538137062 (ebook)
Subjects: LCSH: Libraries—Activity programs—United States. | Libraries—Activity programs—Marketing. | Libraries—Activity programs—Evaluation.
Classification: LCC Z716.33 .F625 2021 (print) | LCC Z716.33 (ebook) | DDC 025.5—dc23
LC record available at https://lccn.loc.gov/2020052316
LC ebook record available at https://lccn.loc.gov/2020052317

CONTENTS

PREFACE	ix
ACKNOWLEDGMENTS	xi
1 PLANNING	1
2 FUNDING	27
3 MARKETING AND PUBLICIZING EVENTS	43
4 EVALUATION AND OUTCOME MEASURES	65
5 REPORTING THE RESULTS	83
6 USING DATA TO INFORM SERVICE PROVISION	97
7 THE LIFE CYCLE OF LIBRARY PROGRAMMING	109
RESOURCES	123
INDEX	127
ABOUT THE AUTHOR	129

PREFACE

Libraries of all types are constantly expanding their services in order to remain responsive to their varied user communities. As part of this expansion, there is an increasing emphasis on providing programs and hosting events; this evolution in services has been met with enthusiasm by library users. In fact, numbers for program attendance in all types of public libraries in the United States (large, small, rural, and urban) increased more than 30 percent nationwide in the decade between 2004 and 2014 (IMLS, 2017). *Great Library Events: From Planning to Promotion to Evaluation* provides a wealth of information on incorporating event and program provision into regular library services. This book is aimed at library managers and programming staff, but will be helpful for anyone responsible for event or program planning in their organization, whether they're new to the task or seasoned professionals.

We begin with the first steps of planning events, from defining the scope and choosing topics to involving staff and moving the plan forward. Chapter 2 continues with finding funding, and focuses on determining needs, crafting a budget, and locating resources. Marketing and publicizing events is the emphasis of chapter 3, which includes getting the word out, marketing on a shoestring, and examples of successful initiatives. Chapter 4 delves into data collection for evaluating the success and impact of programs, followed up in chapter 5 with using data for reporting results and informing stakeholders. Chapter 6 is focused on using evaluation data to inform service provision and keep the program cycle going. The final chapter discusses the life cycle of programs, addresses general environmental sustainability considerations, and then further resources are provided.

PREFACE

During these unusual and unprecedented times, libraries and their ongoing promotion of community growth and connectedness are more important than ever before. This volume is filled with practical examples and tips from practitioners in the field, providing tools to guide informed event planning and intentional program provision with the hope of supporting the incredible work that is happening every day throughout libraries everywhere.

REFERENCE

Institute of Museum and Library Services. (2017, September 14). "IMLS Releases Annual Data and Survey Results of American Public Libraries." Accessed December 14, 2020. https://www.imls.gov/news/imls-releases-annual-data-and-survey-results-american-public-libraries

ACKNOWLEDGMENTS

My sincerest thanks to all the librarians out there who are making their communities stronger, more versatile, and more welcoming places. My gratitude to Charles Harmon, who buoyed me along, and to Erinn Slanina for her helpful support. I would also like to thank GW for their unfailing support throughout the process. Sincere thanks as well to all the contributors—Suzanne Bloom, Vickery Bowles, Erica Brody, Amelia Gibson, Taylor Johnson, Leila Ledbetter, Noah Lenstra, Maggie Melo, David Miller, Lydia Neuroth, and Gwendolyn Reece—for sharing their stories.

1

PLANNING

As part of their educational mission, libraries have long been in the business of hosting events and programs. In fact, programs can be viewed as yet another resource or opportunity that libraries have regularly offered to their communities. Public libraries have been codifying and reporting on such initiatives for some time now. The first issues of the New York Public Library's (NYPL) monthly print publication, *Branch Library News*, from more than a century ago describe a variety of book clubs, exhibits, and meetings that were supported through the library's routine program opportunities (New York Public Library, 1914a–d). Some of the offerings bear some similarity to programs offered by public, academic, and special libraries today.

Examples include:

- Library, literary, and reading clubs
- Debates (the first was "When the Boys' Literary Club of the 115th Street Branch challenged the boys of the Harlem Library League to a trial debate," 1914a, p. 96)
- Illustrated talks on the district's history
- Job talks by school principals for new graduates (separate talks were given to boys and girls)
- Guest speakers, such as authors and a local judge
- Musical programs
- Mothers' clubs
- Exhibits with topics such as child welfare (including books, maps, photographs); Indians in the Southwest (with pottery, baskets, photographs);

CHAPTER 1

and a 350th anniversary celebration of Shakespeare's birth (with rare prints and editions on display)
- English classes
- Neighborhood and civic organization meetings

Even in 1914, the importance of the libraries' connection to community was emphasized. They were considered akin to schools in the movement to make schoolhouses as "civic and social centres [sic] of the community," as they were similarly described to "naturally offer striking opportunities for neighborhood development" (NYPL, 1914e). Along these lines, the branch libraries were depicted as integral "meeting-places" (NYPL, 1914f). The 1913 annual report describes the "frequent and varied use of the branch library as 'the logical meeting-place for clubs and organizations that represent the life of the community,'" and the monthly bulletin reports that "two organizations of physicians held their first meetings in February" (NYPL, 1914g). So, along with their resource and information provision roles, libraries have for more than a century been understood by the public to be places for hosting events and providing community meeting opportunities. Many programs, like children's story time, may not ever be attended by most people, and yet those same people will be vehement supporters of those services. Program events help define the community's values and the library's mission, and bring those two entities closer together. Library events can be bigger than the events themselves.

STARTING THE BALL ROLLING

Defining the Mission, Purpose, and Scope of the Event

As with many endeavors, the first step in event planning is to define the mission and purpose. What is the mission of the event and how does it fit in with the larger library mission? Is the event part of an initiative to promote literacy or lifelong learning? Is it to highlight or promote library resources? Is its purpose to respond to current community challenges? As for scope, will it be targeted to a specific user group, or is the purpose to bring in or reach out to new library users? Will it include other communities or regional and statewide partners? The mission and purpose will then steer the choice of topic and guide decisions about whether this will be a short- or long-term project and whether it will be a one-shot event or ongoing offering (as will the ultimate results of the event). For example, if there is little community interest in the first trial of a program, it may not be worth repeating.

PLANNING

Some purposes are readily defined because of their unique circumstance, such as in the case of special events (e.g., anniversary celebrations) and established programs (e.g., summer reading in public libraries).

The following questions can help to frame the process during the idea formation phase:

- Who is the likely audience?
- What are your goals and objectives?
- Who (if anyone) are likely collaborators?
- When will the event take place, and what are the milestones in between?
- How will you ensure accessibility and inclusivity?

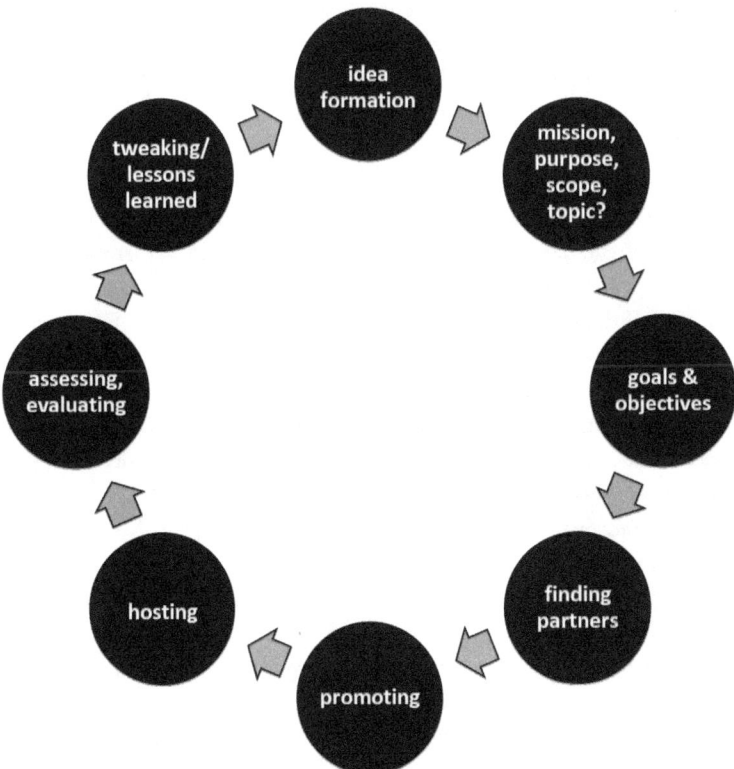

Figure 1.1. Stages of library programs. *Courtesy of the author*

CHAPTER 1

CHOOSING THE TOPIC

Determining Your Audience

The purpose of the program or event will likely determine both the target audience and the specific topic. For instance, if as director of an academic library you have a newly formed collaboration with your student health center, programs might be steered toward issues that are affecting a segment of the student population, such as stress reduction for incoming first-years.

As with collection development and other library activities, responding to community needs and wishes is paramount in terms of library service provision. This dependence on community interest is not only because of attendance; it also influences long-term financial support for the library and staff morale and enthusiasm. But who determines what those community needs are? How are those needs codified? And how are communities' wishes made known?

The Network of the National Library of Medicine (NNLM) describes community engagement as a continuum. At one end are activities that simply make the community aware of services, while at the other end, patrons have leadership responsibilities within the organization.

The NNLM provides a free community engagement toolkit (available at https://nnlm.gov/all-of-us/cp/resource/community-engagement-toolkit) that helps to build upon the already established and direct knowledge of patrons that occurs through regular interaction. The NNLM advocates for using community assessments to better know your audience as a way to ensure programs and services are relevant to the "needs, strengths, and interests of the community." Assessments can also help to identify any gaps in services or community members that are not being regularly reached. The community engagement toolkit provides links to free, readily available resources, such as a Community Assessment Factsheet and a Community Tool Box.

There are also resources for utilizing health statistics in community assessments, such as the County Health Rankings (https://www.countyhealthrankings.org) available from the Robert Wood Johnson Foundation. Using such tools can help to determine what topics current programs and events might cover. For instance, by examining health rankings, you may discover the community has a high rate of a particular health concern and can adapt programming to offer support to address that concern. Once the topic and audience have been determined, it's time to turn to goals and objectives.

Setting Goals and Objectives

There is an abundance of guidance on setting goals and objectives, whether in the business, education, organizational, or general literature. Without going into too much detail here, the key things to keep in mind when setting goals and objectives are to make them clear and make them measurable. The reliable ABCD method of writing learning objectives and learning outcomes can be used as a guide (University of Maryland, 2020).

- A = Audience: Who is the target audience? (e.g., young adults)
- B = Behavior: What will be accomplished? (e.g., attendance; skill acquisition)
  - Should be measurable and observable
  - Use action verbs that describe behaviors
- C = Condition: Under what circumstances will behavior occur? (e.g., "by the end of the program")
- D = Degree: How will behavior need to be performed (how much or how well)? (e.g., "will attend 3 of 5 activities")

So, for example, if one of your overarching goals is to bring more young adults into the library, and you've determined there's interest in this patron group to learn how to juggle, you can offer a juggling workshop with the following objective: *As a result of participating in the Introduction to Juggling workshop (condition), young adult attendees (audience) will explain (behavior) the basic component (degree) of circle juggling.* Setting achievable and measurable goals and objectives is key to determining success and is necessary for a robust evaluation process.

Identifying Partners and Collaborators

Libraries of all types are valued and trusted as institutional and organizational collaborators; collaboration is what libraries do. Partnerships can offer different types of support, such as financial, social network, institutional, in-kind, or resource support. In the academic library setting, collaborations occur across libraries, departments, schools, or campuses and beyond. School librarians' primary interactions are with teachers, though they may collaborate with other schools, across districts, and with public libraries and community organizations. Library science students and students within a subject specialty are often looking for opportunities to help with program or event planning in all types of library settings. In order to gain experience, field studies or internships can offer a mutually beneficial experience and help to launch our next generation of engaged librarians.

Figure 1.2. illustrates the public library's "community constellation of potential health outreach collaborators" for efforts around health promotion, but they can easily apply to any type of collaboration and library (Flaherty, 2018, p. 77).

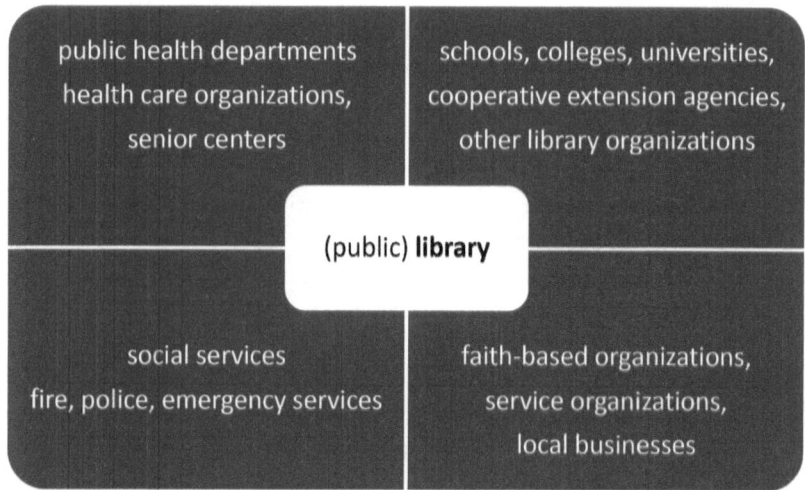

Figure 1.2. Potential community collaborators. *Flaherty, M.G. Promoting Individual and Community Health at the Library. Chicago, IL: ALA, 2018.*

The best way to identify potential partnerships is to be an active member of the community where the library is located. Libraries and library staff are generally highly valued community assets, and as such, opportunities for participation in collaborative or cooperative efforts often arise without solicitation. These opportunities can offer easy options for program support as long as they fit in with the library's goals and mission. For instance, when I worked at the Sidney Memorial Public Library, we were often approached by local service organizations and regularly offered financial support for children's programming. Besides having the resources to support the programs, the library's newly added community room was the best venue in town for large group gatherings. It was a win-win in terms of maximizing community resources.

PLANNING

The Community Toolkit mentioned earlier also provides guidance and tools for working with partners, including a model memorandum of collaboration: Community Toolkit—Collaboration (https://ctb.ku.edu/en/table-of-contents/overview/model-for-community-change-and-improvement/framework-for-collaboration/main).

Tending to inclusion for all community members, no matter the setting, should be addressed from the start. The textbox below by Dr. Amelia Gibson describes how to plan for and ensure accessibility and inclusivity for a range of community members.

WORKING TOWARD INCLUSION

At their best, libraries fulfill their functions as information and technology hubs for communities while demonstrating a liberatory ethic of care—strengthening whole communities by fortifying community bonds and relationships, responding equitably to needs within communities, and not causing harm (e.g., not increasing educational gaps and currently existing disparities in information and technology access; Dutt & Kohfeldt, 2018). Inclusive libraries actively and intentionally recognize the inherent value of all community members and provide equitable support in assessment, planning, programming, policies, and collection development, regardless of political influence or tax contributions. The inverse of inclusive environments—exclusionary environments—are those that, intentionally or unintentionally, ignore the needs of segments of the community, focusing primarily on the loudest and most influential stakeholders. This segment addresses building more inclusive libraries through community assessment and planning. Because marginalization tends to be persistent, pervasive, and structural, I focus on traditionally marginalized groups that often do not have equitable representation in local government, in library administration, or on library boards.

Think about Inclusion from the Start

Library staff and administration who conduct community assessments should include equity and inclusion both as core motivations and as guiding (or organizing) principles for evaluation of library policies, services, collections, and programs. Ideally, inclusive and equitable planning, resource allocation, and program/policy execution will become a normal part of staff and administrative routines. This means engaging in frank and regular discussions about who is marginalized or excluded through policy and programming choices. Consider the following tactics for ensuring that inclusion is a fundamental part of assessment and programming:

- Ask, "Who is *not* here, and why?" rather than surveying regular patrons for satisfaction with current programming.
- Examine library policies (including conduct and borrowing policies) to examine whether the benefits of using the library outweigh the inherent risks. Is the potential for high fines too risky for community members with low incomes?
- Examine the library's formal exclusion records and your local police department records to see what groups of people are asked to leave the library (and are arrested at the library) most frequently, as was done in the Seattle public library (Barnett, 2018). Do your library police or security have a history of conflict with specific portions of your community (e.g., people of color, teens, or community members who are experiencing homelessness)? Be mindful that to some library staff, removing "noisy" or "unruly" patrons might intuitively feel like "safety." Examine how personal discomfort with people from different cultures and people with disabilities can lead to systemic discrimination. Consider inviting members of those groups to help craft more inclusive policies.
- Invest time and money into disability, racial equity, and LGBTQ+ cultural competency (or) training (e.g., SafeZone, available at https://thesafezoneproject.com) for *all* staff.
- Reinforce the importance of disability inclusion (rather than defaulting to segregation) in *all* library programming, while recognizing the affirmative value of affinity spaces and spaces where disabled people can lead without being taken over by nondisabled peers.

Retrofitting inclusion is always more expensive than planning inclusive programs in the first place. It is more productive (and often less time, labor, and resource intensive) to routinely building inclusive and accommodating programs.

Embrace the Diversity of Your Local Community, and Plan and Act Proactively to Meet Their Needs as Individuals and as Groups

While it might be tempting to ignore differences in identity (such as race, gender, sexuality, or disability) and socioeconomic status among community members, understanding how people's experiences and needs differ can help us plan more inclusive services and programming. When we ignore those differences, rather than learning about and embracing them, we often end up unwittingly creating spaces and programs that exclude parts of the community. Here are a few points to consider:

- *Building an inclusive library is about more than just being "good" or kind to everyone—it requires active learning, listening, and systemic changes.* Individual kindness is not enough to build an inclusive library system. Real inclusion first requires us to learn about the experiences, values, and needs of *all* segments of the community (including those who do not visit the library frequently), the issues that are important to them and to their communities, their histories in our local and national communities, and relevant laws (such as the ADA, the Civil Rights Act, and other laws and guidelines). It requires that we enact individual standards for engagement *and* necessary systemic changes to library policy, resource allocation, planning, and programming. Focusing solely on personal self-assessments of individual behavior leaves us vulnerable to our own biases and allows us to dismiss systemic discrimination as a series of individual conflicts (or individual instances of broken rules). We often don't know what we don't know when it comes to inclusion and discrimination, and focusing on individual feelings about kindness and "reasonable" levels of effort for inclusion can lead us to prioritize the preferences and feelings of library staff and administration at the expense of marginalized community members' civil rights. For example, a staff member who is not familiar with the varied functions of service animals or ADA guidelines might assume that it would be reasonable to deny access to a sighted person's service dog based on the possibility that other patrons might have pet allergies. This would be illegal (US Department of Justice, 2010). Beyond being a matter of justice or rights, this type of uninformed and intuitive policy making also hinders disabled people in particular from fully and meaningfully accessible library spaces and resources, as many people do not understand basic disability inclusion, accommodations, or law. This individualistic approach also ignores more systemic damage done when these informal, "intuitive" policies are codified into official library policies, programs, and collections that ignore the needs of traditionally underrepresented community members.
- *Every target audience is made up of many subgroups, and identities overlap and intersect.* When assessing communities and planning for a specific audience, we should consider what subgroups might make up that audience. We each represent many communities and

CHAPTER 1

identities, and different groups of people have different experiences and needs—even when we live in the same geographic communities (Gibson & Hanson-Baldauf, 2019). Sometimes specific portions of an audience have experiences and needs that other parts of that audience do not share (Crenshaw, 1989). For example, when planning an event for "young adults," we should consider that a group made up exclusively of young adult, nondisabled Black Latina/x women would probably have slightly different needs, perspectives, and interests than the same group would if it included disabled participants. Similarly, depending on the location and the nature of the programming, a group of nondisabled white non-Latina/x women might have different concerns, needs, and interests still.

- *Understanding the needs of different parts of your community can help you plan proactively.* Thinking proactively about the needs and interests of different subgroups within your target audience can help you plan ahead for things like translation needs, ensuring a physically accessible space, building an intellectually accessible program (for people of different ages or with intellectual or learning disabilities), accommodating different types of sensory needs, helping you avoid cultural conflicts, and limiting financial or social barriers to participation. Knowing about the different impacts of local and national events on different groups of community members can help us plan programs that might address specific community interests and needs.
- *Inclusion requires understanding* and *informed, equitable action.* Imagine that your library is planning to offer job search training sessions as part of your community programming. An equitable approach to planning would include a demographic assessment to ensure that you understand *who* in your community is unemployed. Are certain racial or ethnic groups overrepresented in this sample? What about disabled people? Undocumented community members? Anyone else? Once you understand who your audience(s) is (or are), you need to educate yourself on how to plan a program that is useful and accessible to these groups. For example, you see that intellectually disabled young adults in your local community have a high unemployment rate, and by talking to a few community members, consulting with local organizations, and doing some reading, you discover that this is partially due to a low success rate with job applications. Understanding this as a need for this specific group could help you plan more effective and inclusive job-searching classes, with the appropriate amount of staffing needed to include participants who might need extra attention, pre-teaching materials for review ahead of time, shorter and more flexible lesson plans, more readable hand-

outs, and guest facilitators from your state's Office for Vocational Rehabilitation, among other things (see Principles of Universal Design, below). The library might decide to advertise to groups that serve that population (e.g., the local Arc, Down syndrome association, or autism society). Without a proper assessment and knowledge about the needs of this portion of the community, the library might have been ill prepared for disabled community members who attempted to participate or might have excluded disabled participants by not making their preparation clear. Identities alone cannot tell us what any individual person might want, like, or dislike, but they can cue us to these sorts of programming needs, cultural norms, and current and historic community concerns. Likewise, understanding and empathizing with community members is not enough to create inclusion—informed action is necessary.

- *Embracing and understanding diversity and planning inclusive programs is a balance* between learning about the lived group experiences and histories of people in your community and engaging with them and learning about their needs as individuals. That balance is easier to maintain if you build inclusive social norms throughout the library.

Inclusion Is an Ongoing Process

Learning about how to build and maintain an inclusive, welcoming library never ends. Communities constantly change and grow, technology and customs change, and we continue to learn about new portions of our local communities. Any change that affects your community members, including large-scale demographic changes, local and national politics, and economic changes, will alter community needs and change how inclusion happens in your library. Sustainable inclusion is based in the recognition that, while some things need to happen as quickly as possible, the learning and development (personal and institutional) that accompany inclusion efforts evolve and grow over time. This process requires a certain level of personal, institutional, and cultural humility (Tervalon & Murray-García, 1998) and willingness to move past (sometimes demoralizing) mistakes in the interest of continued improvement. Intracommunity and subcommunity debates such as the person-first ("person with a disability") versus identity-first ("disabled person") language (Brown, 2011; Haelle, 2019) debate might sometimes be difficult to understand and follow. It will probably be necessary to learn how to listen, follow the lead of local community members, sometimes apologize, and move forward, even in the absence of external praise or applause. This is especially true for organizations that have a history of discrimination and must work to reconcile broken relationships with marginalized community members. Building trusting relationships is a slow process, and once built, those relationships must be maintained over time.

In the Meantime: Principles of Universal Design

Community assessments can help give a rich picture of demographics, practices, and needs within specific communities. Universal design for learning provides general principles for supporting learning among a culturally diverse and neurodiverse group. Universal design is not a panacea and is not a replacement for developing an inclusive and diverse leadership team or for doing community assessment, but it provides a useful starting point for planning and program design. The following guidelines are adapted from the CAST UDL Guidelines (CAST, 2020):

1. *Respect the agency, interests, and needs of your community members as they engage with the library, programming, and materials.*
    a. Find out what programs would be useful for community members by listening to them, rather than prioritizing what is easy for the staff or what the library "has always done."
    b. Allow people freedom and support agency in participation as much as possible. This means really assessing when rules for participation are necessary and when they are more about maintaining control for our own comfort.
    c. Make program goals useful, relevant, salient, and authentic *for your audience* (not necessarily for the library).
    d. Provide the structural support that makes individual coping strategies acceptable, feasible, and effective. Do not demand conformity for its own sake or to appease others' biases (e.g., library staff clearly modeling acceptance of stimming behaviors by autistic community members might reduce stigma among other patrons).
    e. Support self-assessment, autonomous benchmarking, and develop mechanisms for community support.
2. *Use a variety of media/means of representation.*
    a. Try to offer as many alternative formats as possible for any piece of information (e.g., written text/captioning, spoken words, and sign language). Make writing and illustrations simple, short, and clear.
    b. Whenever possible, allow community members to control the formatting or display of information.
    c. Make sure that language is understandable by offering translation whenever possible for spoken and written language (especially

in areas with large multilingual or non-English-speaking populations). Offer sign language and closed captioning whenever possible. Remember that American Sign Language (ASL) and written American English are two different languages—many deaf people who use ASL cannot read written English, and vice versa (Hrastinski & Wilbur, 2016).
d. Provide background information and materials for previewing whenever possible. Handouts or videos providing information about the topic, the program plan, and the library space can help disabled people adequately prepare to participate in public programs.
e. Support comprehension as much as possible, including explicitly (and sometimes repetitively) highlighting "big ideas," guiding reasoning, information processing, and generalization of concepts.
3. *Provide many options for community members to express themselves.*
a. Offer many options for movement and many acceptable "ways of being" in the space. For example, do not mandate that all participants sit in chairs or on a rug for the entire program. Allow them to move as they see fit.
b. Offer as free access to (and support for) assistive technology and tools, including use of multiple media for self-expression.
c. Offer multiple levels of support for individual and group practice, management of information, self-monitoring (and voluntary group monitoring), increased agency in goal setting, and demonstration of goals.

The full CAST guidelines can be found on the organization's website (http://udlguidelines.cast.org/). Additional tools for assessment of library programming for disabled community members and understanding basic disability issues in libraries can be found at https://cedi.unc.edu/toolkit/.

There is no way to completely ensure inclusion because communities are constantly growing, learning, and changing. Just as we must continually engage in self-reflection and assessment of our personal intentions and behaviors, libraries must continue to assess community needs and institutional actions to ensure continued provision of equitable and genuinely supportive services to all segments of their communities.

REFERENCES

Barnett, Erica. (2018, August 22). *People of Color, Especially Children, Most Likely to be Asked to Leave Seattle Libraries*. South Seattle Emerald. https://southseatt

CHAPTER 1

leemerald.com/2018/08/22/people-of-color-especially-children-most-likely-to-be-asked-to-leave-seattle-libraries/
Brown, L. X. Z. (2011). *Identity-First Language*. Autistic Self Advocacy Network. https://autisticadvocacy.org/about-asan/identity-first-language/
CAST. (2020). "UDL: The UDL Guidelines." http://udlguidelines.cast.org/
Crenshaw, K. (1989). "Demarginalizing the Intersection of Race and Sex: A Black Feminist Critique of Antidiscrimination Doctrine, Feminist Theory and Antiracist Politics." *University of Chicago Legal Forum, 1989*, 139.
Dutt, A., & Kohfeldt, D. (2018). "Towards a Liberatory Ethics of Care Framework for Organizing Social Change." *Journal of Social and Political Psychology*, 6(2), 575–90. https://doi.org/10.5964/jspp.v6i2.909
Gibson, A. N., & Hanson-Baldauf, D. (2019). "Beyond Sensory Story Time: An Intersectional Analysis of Information Seeking among Parents of Autistic Individuals." *Library Trends*, 67(3), 550–575. https://doi.org/10.1353/lib.2019.0002
Haelle, T. (2019, July 31). "Identity-First vs. Person-First Language Is an Important Distinction. Association of Health Care Journalists." https://healthjournalism.org/blog/2019/07/identity-first-vs-person-first-language-is-an-important-distinction/
Hrastinski, I., & Wilbur, R. B. (2016). "Academic Achievement of Deaf and Hard-of-Hearing Students in an ASL/English Bilingual Program." *Journal of Deaf Studies and Deaf Education*, 21(2), 156–70. https://doi.org/10.1093/deafed/env072
Tervalon, M., & Murray-García, J. (1998). "Cultural Humility versus Cultural Competence: A Critical Distinction in Defining Physician Training Outcomes in Multicultural Education." *Journal of Health Care for the Poor and Underserved*, 9(2), 117–25. https://doi.org/10.1353/hpu.2010.0233
US Department of Justice. (2010). *ADA 2010 Revised Requirements: Service Animals*. https://www.ada.gov/service_animals_2010.htm

Amelia N. Gibson, PhD, MLIS
Assistant Professor, School of Information and Library Science
Director, CEDI Lab (https://cedi.unc.edu)
University of North Carolina at Chapel Hill

Using Ready-Made Themes

There are numerous approaches and resources that may guide program provision, such as the use of themes around certain dates or months. *Chase's Calendar of Events*, available from Rowman & Littlefield, is a popular resource and standard reference tool for using dates to commemorate or recognize a wide variety of groups and subject areas. Consider having library staff make choices and propose programming opportunities based on their interests.

Another ready-made resource for public libraries is from the NNLM, which provides resources that align with National Health Observances (NHO) throughout the calendar year (available at https://nnlm.gov/all-of-us/national-health-observances). Beyond the resources for NHO programs, the NNLM also offers other program kits, including the community engagement toolkit described above, resources on digital health literacy, and evaluation tools (http://nnlm.gov/all-of-us/resources).

Table 1.1 provides a start for possible ideas for creating programs using such monthly themed guides.

Table 1.1. Monthly Program Topics

Month	Possible Topics
January	National Cervical Cancer Awareness Month
	National Mentoring Month
	Slavery & Human Trafficking Prevention Month
February	American Heart Month
	Black History Month
	National Bird Feeding Month
March	National Colon Cancer Awareness Month
	Nutrition Month
	Women's History Month
April	Autism Awareness Month
	Cancer Control Month
	Financial Literacy Month
	Jazz Appreciation Month
	National Arab American Heritage Month
	National Library week
	National Poetry Month
	School Library Month
	Sexual Assault Awareness Month
May	Asia Pacific American Heritage Month
	Employee Health & Fitness Month
	Haitian Heritage Month
	Jewish American Heritage Month
	Mental Health Awareness Month
	National Bike Month
	National Pet Month
	National Physical Fitness & Sports Month
June	African American Music Appreciation Month
	LGBTQ+ Pride Month
	Men's Health Month
	National Safety Month
	Rainbow Book Month
July	National Ice Cream Month
	UV Safety Month
August	Children's Eye Health & Safety Month
	National Breastfeeding Awareness Month
	National Immunization Awareness Month

(continued)

CHAPTER 1

Table 1.1. Monthly Program Topics

September	Banned Books Week
	Library Card Sign-up Month
	National Preparedness Month
	National Yoga Month
October	Breast Cancer Awareness Month
	Filipino American History Month
	Health Literacy Month
	Italian American Heritage and Culture Month
	LGBTQ+ History Month
	National Arts and Humanities Month
	National Bullying Prevention Month
	National Disability Employment Awareness Month
	National Hispanic Heritage Month (9/15–10/15)
	National Pizza Month
November	Diabetes Month
	Native American Indian/Alaska Native Heritage Month
	Picture Book Month
December	Safe Toys & Gifts Month

So, to celebrate National Bike Month in May, the library could follow the lead of the Farmville Public Library in eastern North Carolina, which holds regular "bike clinics," partnering with a local cycling group, bike shop, and the Farmville police to promote using bicycles for exercise and transportation. The library provides a range of activities, including bike repair instruction, free helmet giveaways, and a bike course set up in the library parking lot. The clinics draw attendees from all over the region and are adaptable to accommodate for social distancing. At the most recent clinic (September 19, 2020) seventeen bicycles were serviced, and twelve helmets were given away. Three bike mechanics volunteered their time, and the library director changed a few inner tubes as well. This was the fourth time the event was offered, and the library is already planning the next one. A local reporter took photos of the event, and the library posted the lively pictures on its social media account.

The library hopes to add another component to the program, offering to repair bicycles that the local police department acquires (for various reasons), and then giving them away to folks who need them. As of late September 2020, the police department had thirteen bicycles of varying sizes, all in need of basic maintenance. The library staff are currently working on a way to determine a way to identify the folks most in need of them.

CONTINGENCY PLANNING

As this book is going to press, we are in the throes of the global COVID-19 pandemic. The primary lesson learned during these unprecedented times is the need for flexibility and adaptability, no matter how carefully we have planned. The Programming in Action feature below describes the process of converting and adapting the delivery of a program that was designed and planned before the pandemic upended our regular, time-tested approaches to program provision.

PROGRAMMING IN ACTION: ZINE-MAKING WORKSHOP AT CAMERON VILLAGE REGIONAL LIBRARY

From June 2019 through July 2020, I served as a library intern for Wake County Public Libraries (WCPL) at the Cameron Village Regional Library (CAM) branch. One of my responsibilities included planning and delivering my own public program, so I decided to create a zine-making workshop. I designed a twenty-minute introduction to cover some background information on zines followed by an hour-long hands-on workshop for participants to create a personal zine. As I originally designed it for presentation in April 2020, the theme was: Zines: What Is Your Story?

Why Zines at Cameron Village?

1. Welcoming a new audience
   One of the goals for my program was to create an experience that I myself might enjoy, assuming it would also appeal to my millennial peers. CAM has traditionally excelled in gaining the participation of the older demographic. The library is less than two miles from the campus of North Carolina State University (NCSU), and while students frequent the library for study spaces and research support, they are less likely to participate in adult services programs.
2. Using a familiar model
   The style of the program mimicked a model that WCPL was already utilizing. WCPL holds monthly "Craft-It" programs led by a professional librarian who explains how to make a craft and then lets participants use the majority of their time to independently create. WCPL's "Write-It" program follows a similar format in which a guest speaker (typically a local author) introduces a focus for writing and participants are given an opportunity to practice. I wanted the zine-making workshop to be a combination of these two programs: a creative outlet for telling one's story.

3. Zines are right up my alley
Zines are historically and currently associated with documenting and giving voice to groups underrepresented in mainstream media. Today, many libraries and archives have recognized the importance of preserving these materials in order to tell a more accurate and empowering story of marginalized communities. I am an archivist by training and experience, and it was through archive work that I developed a passion for preserving and sharing stories of people that have historically been denied their voice through mainstream channels. I liked that zines allowed me to mix my passions with a new outlet.

Adapting with COVID-19

As COVID-19 became a reality, WCPL decided to close all library branches to the public as of March 16, 2020. My supervisors and I decided to respond in two different ways to the cancellation of all public programming, which included the cancellation of my zine-making workshop. First, I planned to move forward with holding the workshop at the library, but instead, I would invite a small number of library staff. Second, I decided to create an online static resource that would replicate certain elements of my in-person workshop. For both contingency plans, it was important for me to consider my initial motivations for conducting the program:

1. The audience
2. The unique ability of zines to tell underrepresented stories

The two contingency plans should work in concert!

In-Person Staff Workshop

When shifting to a staff workshop, audience was my first factor to consider. I no longer had direct access to the public, so I needed to explore how I could help my colleagues reproduce this work effectively in the future when in-person programming was again permitted. I decided to look beyond the staff in the adult services department and consider the youth services (YS) librarians who work with teens. While youth were not my target audience, I knew that YS librarians would have valuable insight for program adaptation and how to connect with younger generations. High schoolers are an underreached population at CAM.

I identified my workshop with staff as a training opportunity. I decided to spend more time on the introduction of zines and I enhanced the PowerPoint slides by including an interesting quote about the ability of zines

PLANNING

to empower creators. It was important for my librarians to know the *why* of this programming. Just because I was presenting to staff didn't mean I couldn't bring up hard subjects. I focused attention on the power of zines to bring voice to marginalized communities. I encouraged staff to consider who they are as people and what makes them unique in the same way I would've encouraged a more public audience.

One of the biggest changes I made to the in-person workshop was to provide the option to focus one's zine on documenting their COVID-19 experience. I aimed to balance this with my desire that the workshop be a stress-reducing event. I liked the idea of a protected hour of time for participants to allow their minds to wander, creatively liberated from the burdens of work, home life, and anxieties caused by the recent global health pandemic. However, I also recognized that others might benefit from the opportunity to vent about their experience quarantining and social distancing. As an archivist, I couldn't overlook the opportunity to invite participants to engage with this unique time and reflect. I added two slides into my PowerPoint presentation with questions to consider around quarantine and a few examples of other archiving efforts by universities and public libraries. I expressed the importance of preserving personal histories, which reinforced one of my initial motivations for introducing zines: their unique ability to tell personal stories.

Generating staff interest during a time of social distancing was challenging. I needed to be respectful of concerns and I tried to alleviate fears by explaining the precautions I was taking well in advance of the workshop via e-mail. In addition to thoroughly wiping down tables and having cleaning supplies on hand, I also limited the number of people in the room to ten, spread out tables and chairs, and provided each station with its own materials. Limiting participants to ten meant that I had to be willing to offer more than one session of the workshop if the demand was high. I encouraged participants to bring their own personal protective equipment. In short, the preparation doubled the time required of a traditional program.

Conducting this workshop with librarians was a valuable opportunity to collect feedback from colleagues. I continued with my original plans for assessment, which included an exit ticket asking participants to reflect on (1) their favorite part of the program and (2) what could be improved. I also used our share-out time as observation. I noted what participants focused on when showcasing their zines. This helped me to understand what they liked about the creation process and what was less important to them. For example, most participants shared incomplete zines and indicated verbally and in their exit tickets that they would have liked more time to create. If I did this program again, I would make it two full hours, dedicating at least an hour and a half to creating.

CHAPTER 1

Online Resource

Audience was once again an influential factor as I considered adapting a traditional in-person public program to the online space. I wanted something flashy and robust, with images, videos, and links that appealed to a millennial audience. I wanted a platform that reflected the cool and cutting-edge nature of zines. I was fortunate that my supervisor permitted me to utilize Google Sites, which is malleable, interesting, and intuitive.

There are plenty of well-vetted zine resources out there already, many of which have been created by experts in zine communities or by academic and public librarians. I didn't want to reinvent the wheel. I needed to engage the interest of librarians at WCPL and those in our immediate community by presenting them with a well-vetted guide that spoke to their specific needs and context. For this reason, I began to understand the online resource as a staff toolkit in addition to being a site utilized by the general public. I included the PowerPoint slides from my staff workshop as well as a Google Doc of my program outline with the anticipation it could be adapted for future programs both at my own institution and beyond.

I also decided to include some results of the workshop on the site to motivate librarians and others to experiment. The results illustrate the power of feedback for our public programs and assessment resonates with librarians. I included a short narrative (in my own words) of one participant's expressed feedback and included a quote: "Yes, I enjoyed the workshop; it was interesting and challenging; there're so many elements and such a scope of opportunity for creative expression and reflection." With participants' permission, I used their original content: images from the workshop and staff-created zines.

Without the ability to engage in meaningful dialogue with the public face-to-face, I had to consider ways I would do this effectively on Google Sites. For example: What sources would I use to evoke deep consideration of these topics? How could I group things together so that they made a central point? It probably goes without saying that elements such as an organized and clean layout with well-vetted sources and citations is a must. I decided to make a section on the first page dedicated to further reading about zines on marginalized histories. When pointing to academic and public library collections on zines, I highlighted robust and thoughtful collections that had championed social justice issues and centered the needs and interests of their zine creators and donors. I also pointed to zine LibGuides, many of which provide suggestions on teaching and conducting research with zines. In the absence of having these conversations in person, I wanted to encourage my readers to engage with the controversial topics that define zine culture.

I also needed to gain the trust of my reading audience, primarily librarians. I am not an expert on zines, therefore it was appropriate and necessary for me to take cues from other LibGuides and library websites about zines. For example, I compiled a zine reading list using suggestions from LibGuides produced by public and academic libraries. I cross-referenced these lists with the tools the public library uses every day, such as Goodreads and NoveList. Without the ability to provide in-person reader's advisory, it became all the more important to demonstrate to both librarians and patrons that I was using trusted tools familiar and accessible to them. My reading list included:

- *Whatcha Mean, What's a Zine?* by Esther Watson and Mark Todd
- *The Book of Zines: Readings from the Fringe*, edited by Chip Rowe
- *Girl Zines: Making Media, Doing Feminism*, by Alison Piepmeier
- *Zine Scene: Do It Yourself Guide to Zines*, by Francesca Lia Block and Hillary Carlip
- *Notes from the Underground: Zines and the Politics of Underground Culture*, by Stephen Duncombe

Roll with It!

The great part about zines as a medium is that they are intentionally imperfect, nonconformist, and homegrown. Embrace the opportunity to be flexible and have something not go according to plan! This lesson was by far the most rewarding piece for me in the midst of the global health pandemic. There is always opportunity for growth!

Lydia Neuroth, MSLS
Holleman Intern for Wake County Public Libraries, June 2019–June 2020

In the next Programming in Action example in this chapter, Dr. Maggie Melo provides a comprehensive template on how to plan and present a remote makerspace workshop.

PROGRAMMING IN ACTION: HOW TO PLAN A REMOTE MAKERSPACE WORKSHOP

Makerspaces are becoming familiar additions to public and academic libraries. Often the word "makerspace" conjures up images of 3D printers, wide-open layouts, and innovative spaces that are abuzz with people and whirring machines. While this is common, makerspaces are more

CHAPTER 1

than spaces dedicated to the latest technologies: Makerspaces support collaboration, supportive risk-taking, and the building-out of ideas. These values undergird many makerspaces and, by extension, maker workshops. Resources to guide face-to-face makerspace workshops are abundant. This guide focuses on planning for remote makerspace workshops.

Planning for a remote makerspace workshop reminds us that, for many of us, the home was our first makerspace. Makerspace workshops vary in terms of content and materials needed, but they often ask users to think creatively and resourcefully with what is available to them. A makerspace workshop often begins with a task or objective and typically ends with the creation of a viable artifact. Remote programming could provide synchronous and asynchronous workshops. For users without internet access or who prefer to make sans screen, you could send lesson plans via e-mail or surface mail. Specifically, the guidelines below outline some pointers to consider when planning for remote makerspace workshops.

Create a Lesson Plan

Include the following details in your lesson plan:

- Identify your audience (e.g., LGBTQ+ teens or parents interested in entrepreneurship).
- Decide the makerspace workshop's duration.
    - *Tip:* Be mindful of how long a remote makerspace workshop is. After an hour, users tend to experience screen fatigue.
- Decide the workshop date or dates. Will this be a one-time workshop, or will it be a workshop series? For example, a makerspace workshop series could focus on upcycling. One week it's turning soup cans into flowerpots; the next week it's turning plastic cartons into lamps.
- Outline the learning objectives.
- List the needed materials.
    - Be flexible. Encourage participants to use whatever materials they have available. Some prompts for inspiration:
        - Prototype an object that solves a common household problem with items that all start with the letter *P*: paper, play dough, pencils, pastry flour, plastic, etc.
        - Tell a story with found objects. Walk around your house and find four items you can construct with. Now go outside and find four items you can construct with as well.
- Outline the step-by-step instructions.

Once the lesson plan is crafted it can be applied to the following remote workshop approaches below.

PLANNING

Synchronous Telepresence Workshop

Some considerations:

- Ensure you have adequate lighting, a stable internet connection, and an operational microphone and camera before the workshop starts.
- Enlist a coteacher to focus on the technical side of the workshop: e.g., "If you have any questions or problems, please e-mail Jess for help."
  - Ensure parameters are in place to prevent uninvited participants ("Zoom bombers") and to remove participants if needed.
  - The coteacher will monitor the chat, post links, and troubleshoot issues that come up.
- Be mindful of the camera's perspective. It could be difficult to have both your face and your hands in the same frame at all times.
- *Advanced tip:* If possible, have one camera pointed toward your face and another that provides a view of what your hands are doing/making. You can get a tripod for a tablet or phone to use for the secondary camera.

Asynchronous Video Workshop

Some considerations:

- Apply the pointers from the previous section where applicable.
- Use the lesson plan as a guide for your video. This will help cut down on retakes.
- Start the video with an introduction of yourself, what the workshop will cover, and the learning objectives of the workshop.
- Provide a high-level look at the needed materials after providing the workshop introduction. Show users the materials.
- Add subtitles to your video to make it as accessible as possible.
- If possible, create transitions, provide voice-over narration, and edit the video to make it as clear as possible for users.
- Post the video and share the link (and lesson plan!) with users.

This high-level framework was developed with a remote audience in mind, but many of these pointers can be applied to face-to-face workshops too. Have fun!

Marijel (Maggie) Melo, PhD
Assistant Professor
School of Information and Library Science
University of North Carolina at Chapel Hill

CHAPTER 1

MOVING THE PLAN AHEAD

Diving into Next Steps

Once you have:

- determined the purpose for/of the program or event;
- defined the audience;
- set goals and objectives;
- identified collaborators;
- assessed your space options and assets;
- settled on a date;
- and crafted an accessibility and inclusivity plan,

it's now time to create the timeline and task list and determine milestones.

Christensen (n.d.) outlines eight steps to building a project management timeline, including tasks and milestone markers:

1. Write a project scope statement.
2. Create a work breakdown structure.
3. Break each work package into tasks.
4. Determine project dependencies.
5. Determine total time needed for each task.
6. Identify resource availability.
7. Identify important milestones.
8. Build your timeline.

This can be done using very simple, readily available tools (e.g., Table and/or SmartArt Graphic basic timeline function in Word or Timeline templates in PowerPoint) from open-access templates to sophisticated software, depending on organizational preferences, tools, and resources. Sharing of documents can happen in a variety of ways as well (e.g., Microsoft OneDrive and Teams, Google Docs and Google Drive or Dropbox), again depending on organizational preferences, tools, and resources. Tasks can be readily divided among team members to maximize input and minimize workloads.

PLANNING

RECAP

This chapter addressed the planning phase of program and event provision. Beginning with defining the purpose and ensuring it is in keeping with the library's mission and using the logical steps of determining the audience, setting goals and objectives, identifying collaborators, including an accessibility plan, and leaving room for flexibility and adaptability will help to ensure a successful path ahead.

REFERENCES

Christensen, Emily. (n.d.). "8 Steps to Build a Project Management Timeline." Lucidchart. Accessed July 25, 2020. https://www.lucidchart.com/blog/8-steps-to-build-a-project-management-timeline

Flaherty, M. G. (2018). *Promoting Individual and Community Health at the Library.* Chicago: American Library Association.

New York Public Library. (1914a). "Library Reading Clubs." *Branch Library News,* 1(7), 95–96.

New York Public Library. (1914b). "Child Welfare Exhibit of the Kips Bay Neighborhood Association." *Branch Library News,* 1(2), 15.

New York Public Library. (1914c). "Shakespeare Celebration." *Branch Library News,* 1(5), 63.

New York Public Library. (1914d). "Teaching English in the Branch Library." *Branch Library News,* 1(4), 46.

New York Public Library. (1914e). "Libraries and Neighborhood Development." *Branch Library News,* 1(9), 123.

New York Public Library. (1914f). "The Branch Library as a Meeting-Place." *Branch Library News,* 1(3), 32.

New York Public Library. (1914g). "Extracts from the Annual Report." *Branch Library News,* 1(4), 47.

University of Maryland, University Libraries Research Guides. (2020, April 20). "ABCD Method: An Introduction." Accessed July 26, 2020. https://lib.guides.umd.edu/c.php?g=598357&p=4144007

FUNDING

Once the planning phase has been initiated and the goals and objectives have been determined for the program or event (as described in chapter 1), the next stage is to determine funding needs and procurement of resources. Many libraries and organizations already have a dedicated budget for programs; thus, this phase may differ according to budget structure and funding arrangements, as described in more detail below. No matter where the money comes from, it will likely be necessary to create a program budget. This chapter includes examples of different kinds of programs and budgets, depending on funding levels and types of events. It continues with identifying funding opportunities, from Friends groups to foundations to government agencies. Descriptions of low-cost options and using local resources round out this chapter on funding.

DETERMINING FUNDING NEEDS

Categories of Needs

There are a number of things to consider at the outset with regard to resource needs for hosting programs or events, and these considerations are likely to be similar in different library settings. Is the goal of the program to attract new library users, to highlight services, or both? Will the event be a stand-alone program, or will it be an ongoing offering? Will the event necessitate an outside speaker, and if so, will it require a larger venue than the library can provide? Are there external resources, such as an event-planning committee in the organization whom you can enlist for support? If the event is supported or sponsored by

CHAPTER 2

an outside authority, will it require further accountability in terms of reporting? For instance, a full-blown anniversary celebration or gala event that involves the larger town or institution will entail more extensive planning and input from more stakeholders and likely will necessitate more funds and resources.

Primary categories of potential resource needs to consider during the preliminary planning and funding consideration for any type of event include:

- Staff
  - Are there dedicated staff?
  - Can volunteers assist with efforts?
- Space
  - Does the library have the needed space on-site?
    - If there is not enough space, should you still consider hosting?
      - If there is not enough space, is a partnership viable?
      - If there is not enough space, is there a low-cost alternative in the community?
      - Are toilet facilities, fire code constraints, heating or ventilation capacities sufficient for the expected attendees?
  - Is parking readily available?
  - Is extra security needed?
  - Accessibility
    - Is the space ADA compliant?
    - Is the venue accessible by public transportation?
- Fees for speaker, performer, permits, etc.
  - Is there dedicated funding readily available?
    - Are alternative sources feasible for the time frame (e.g., grant funding)?
  - Is it necessary to charge an admission fee to supplement funding?
    - Does this jibe with the library's mission?
    - Will you have a mechanism to admit participants who don't have the ability to pay?
- Marketing and promotion
  - What virtual and physical outlets are available?
  - Will extra staff time be needed for these efforts?
  - Is there dedicated funding for materials and printing costs?
  - Is there dedicated funding for advertising costs?
  - Are there community radio/television/websites/social media or other free advertising outlets that can be used?
- Supplies
  - What supplies (if any) are needed?

- Refreshments
  - Will refreshments be necessary?
    - Who will provide them?
    - Are there restrictions (e.g., from grant funder) on using funds?
    - Are there dietary considerations (e.g., food allergies of participants)?

Preliminary planning will entail consideration of all of these factors. Table 2.1 uses the different categories to depict different levels of resources for hosting a program or event, depending on expectations, funding levels, and available resources.

Table 2.1. Example of Preliminary Funding Planning Template of Consideration, Range of Expectations and Needs

	No Dedicated Funds	Little or Limited Funds	Sky Is the Limit
Facility	Library meeting room	Local public meeting venue	Local place of interest (e.g., museum)
Host/Speaker	Library staff member	Local educator	National expert
Marketing	Library venues	Local media	National media
Resources	Collected locally	Local business donations	Purchase outright
Refreshments	Friends hospitality group	Local catering venue	High-end catering venue

Table 2.2 provides a sample plan, using table 2.1 as a template, for a public library program on climate change.

Table 2.2. Example of Funding Planning for a Public Library Program on Climate Change

	No Dedicated Funds	Little or Limited Funds	Sky Is the Limit
Facility	Library meeting room	University auditorium	Regional conference center
Host/Speaker	Show movie	Environmental science professor	Al Gore or Greta Thunberg
Marketing	Library venues	Local media outlets	National advertising campaign
Resources	Library promotional materials	Local donations of reusable water bottles	Purchase carbon offset credits for participants
Refreshments	None	Local farmers' market	Farm-to-table caterers

CHAPTER 2

To make these concepts tangible and to better understand the nature of programs and their costs and needs, I looked at the top one hundred hits from a Bing search on "library program discusses climate change" and the top one hundred Google hits on "library program climate change." (Searches were performed June 16, 2019.) This topic was picked as being likely to be of interest in academic, special, and public libraries.

While the lion's share of hits were about library holdings or events that were not library centered, of the twenty-five library-centered events or initiatives on climate change that were identified, seventeen took place in the library, none were events at another location, and eight were digital or online opportunities. Ten of the hits were about public libraries (involving fifty-nine library outlets), seven were in academic libraries, two were in other libraries, and six were online sites. No mention of food, prizes, awards, or items that cost money were present in the twenty-five articles or announcements. In two events, the speaker or host was from within the institution (one was a faculty member at a university and one was a library staff member who had won an award related to climate change), twelve were outside speakers, one was a multilibrary book club event, and ten were films or online courses or products.

This small peek into library programming suggests that the speaker is likely to either be a meaningful part of the expenses or, as the focus of most program descriptions, will determine the draw and guide the logic and justification for expenditures. For example, Al Gore's address at the 2010 American Library

Figure 2.1. Photo of US Embassy in Burkina Faso program on climate change. *Courtesy of US Embassy Ouagadougou, Burkina Faso; used with permission*

Association Midwinter Meeting certainly incurred security costs, perhaps more than the security costs involved in the US Embassy Library in Burkina Faso inviting schoolchildren in to watch a TED Talk on climate change (United States Embassy, Burkina Faso, 2017), which in turn was certainly more than the Oakland Library's book club event to discuss the book *Being the Change: Live Well and Spark a Climate Revolution*, by Peter Kalmus. Costs of security, food and beverage, fire code compliance, bathroom needs, and other related issues are all likely determined by some combination of the draw of the speaker, the physical setting, and historical levels of engagement.

CRAFTING A BUDGET

Program Budgets

Program budgets are commonly used for planning specific projects; this type of budget approach usually includes expenses and revenues for one project or program only. Revenues for other projects or programs are not included or mixed in with this approach. Because program budgets allow resources to be dedicated to a project, they can help monitor the specific performance of that project, help guide or inspire conversations with boards or philanthropists, and in turn increase accountability of the overall budget. Another advantage of a program budget approach is the ability to determine where more funds are needed and where costs can be reduced. Program budgets aid in setting program priorities, future planning, and identifying how programs are related to organizational goals. There are disadvantages to this type of budget approach as well, including the high level of detailed information needed to craft such a budget, challenges of overlap between budget categories, managerial oversight time, and challenges due to necessary changes in funding amounts over time.

Table 2.3 is an example of a simple program budget for a summer reading program in a public library. Some costs are covered through dedicated funding in the library budget and are supplied through the Children's Department budget. These include advertising, a portion of funding for performers (the remainder is supplied through grant funds), staff salary, benefits, and indirect costs. Indirect costs are costs that are not identified with a specific organizational activity or project but are incurred for the benefit of projects and other activities (National Institutes of Health, 2019). Examples of indirect costs include facility costs, utilities, equipment depreciation, and legal and accounting fees. Printing and prizes will be donated by local area businesses, and the library's Friends group will supply refreshments for all of the programs.

Table 2.3. Example of a Simple Program Budget for a Summer Reading Program in a Public Library

Resource	Estimated Cost	Funded by
Advertising	$750	Children's Dept. budget
Printing	$500	Local business
Prizes	$950	Local businesses
Performers	3 @$500 each = $1,500	Children's Dept. budget; grants
Refreshments	$400	Friends hospitality group
Staff Time	10 hours/week for 12 weeks; @$34/hour = $4,080	Children's Dept. budget
Staff Benefits	35% of salary (prorated); $1,428	Children's Dept. budget
Indirect Costs	Overhead for facility (prorated); 120 hours = $1,430	Library budget
Total	$11,038	All categories
Total Costs to Library	$9,188	Library and Children's Dept.

Tools such as Microsoft Excel provide easy-to-use templates for tracking income and expenses for all types of event budgets.

PROGRAMMING IN ACTION: CELEBRATION OF ONE HUNDRED YEARS OF AVIATION

When I interviewed for a position as the director of a small, rural public library in 2002, I noted with some interest the prominent display of an aircraft magneto in the library's one quiet area, the Swiss Room. Magnetos are used in piston engines to fire an aircraft's spark plugs. I learned during my staff-guided tour that aviation was the lifeblood of the village where the library was located. In the 1920s, the Scintilla Magneto Company (a Swiss company) started a manufacturing plant in the village, and in fact Charles Lindbergh's plane, the *Spirit of St. Louis*, sported a Scintilla magneto. Scintilla was purchased by Bendix Aviation Corporation in 1929 and became one of the first nationally known companies in the county and region. Toward the end of World War II there were nearly nine thousand workers at the Bendix plant, and the Bendix magneto was used in more than 60 percent of US Army fighter planes; estimates say the plant produced magnetos for almost 150,000 different aircraft (Quality Aircraft Accessories, n.d.). In 1951, the *Saturday Evening Post* published the article "The Village We Can't Do Without," which chronicled the history of the company.

FUNDING

Figure 2.2. Cover of *Saturday Evening Post*, March 3, 1951, in which the village of Sidney was featured. *Courtesy of the author*

Upon his death, one of the retirees from Bendix left a significant gift to the library for a capital campaign in the 1990s. His generous contribution resulted in extensive renovations, including the addition of a large community meeting room named in his honor. The Bendix Corporation eventually became Amphenol Aerospace, which is still a major employer in the area. The small village (population approximately 4,000 in 2002) also boasts a somewhat busy municipal airport. Given that my hiring in June 2002 came shortly before the anniversary of the Wright brothers' first flight (December 17, 1903), and the importance of aviation to the village and the library, it seemed that celebrating one hundred years of flight would be a worthy programming endeavor.

Planning started at a regular staff meeting in late 2002, where I first proposed the idea of introducing a series of programs to celebrate the history of aviation. Most staff members were enthusiastic about the proposal, though one or two expressed skepticism, with comments like, "Those rich people who fly, they don't use the library. Why should we bother? They're not our patrons." Nonetheless, we started brainstorming low-cost programs that could reach all age groups in the community. That first discussion yielded ideas about displays and activities, how to involve the airport, possible speakers, and getting the word out. Enthusiasm for the proposal grew

CHAPTER 2

over time. One staff member's husband had a small plane; he donated his time and resources and offered to take staff for a short airplane ride to build excitement about the upcoming celebration. Eighty percent of the staff took him up on the offer.*

Events kicked off in earnest in summer 2003, when a local remote-control airplane enthusiast offered to hang two of his home-built planes in the library lobby for display. One of these was a stunning one-third scale replica of a 1917 Sopwith Camel with a nine-foot wingspan. I can still hear echoes of the squeals of delight from young children when they spied those massive "toy planes" hanging from the beams. The regional newspaper covered the story with a front-page photo. During the next five months, we offered a wide variety of activities and events, such as story time themes dedicated to flying, paper airplane workshops, and a flight simulator program on one of the library's computers (donated by one of the staff's friends) for all ages to try. We also sponsored an essay contest for our local middle schoolers. Every entrant received an aviation patch (purchased through dedicated funding for promotional materials) upon submission of their essay. Entries were judged by the retired middle school principal (who donated her time), and first prize was an airplane ride at the local airport (donated by the local flight instructor, who had a commercial pilot's license with all the legal protections it afforded). Second and third prizes were gift cards from a local store (donated by the local businesses). There was a reception at the library for all entrants (staff volunteered to provide refreshments, including cookies in the shape of airplanes), and the three prize winners read their essays out loud. This event, too, was covered by the local newspaper, with a photo of all the students together holding an airplane propeller (on loan from a local collector).

For Halloween that year, I dressed up as Amelia Earhart and delivered fliers for our events to the local airport. Our dedicated program series took place every two weeks from early November to the final celebration on December 17. Speakers included the remote-control plane hobbyist and an Amphenol retiree who flew in World War II and was a master flight mechanic who had maintained the "flying White House"—the president's plane. The retiree's session broke the record for program attendees up to that time. We also showed a variety of films for all age groups related to flight. We had many artifacts from local residents on display throughout the library, and we tucked bookmarks on aviation and our programs into circulating books over the course of our celebration.

While these efforts did involve a considerable amount of staff time and planning, actual costs to the library were minimal. For promotion of the programs, we used our usual venues, which at the time were posters throughout the neighboring communities, our monthly newsletter, and our regular weekly column in the regional newspaper. The fact that other area newspapers covered our events was an added bonus that brought patronage from a wider geographic area than usual. The speakers and pilots volunteered their time, as did other participants, such as the judge of the essay contest and folks who put together displays. Local businesses donated prizes. The only purchases made by the library were the aviation patches, which cost around $50 and came out of the promotional items budget line. Taken altogether, the programs brought hundreds of participants to the library over the five-month period. The spirit that came to life in the community around aviation was priceless.

* A lively discussion at the monthly board meeting centered on liability concerns determined that this offer could not be considered as a library-sponsored activity; thus staff arranged this activity on their own time.

Reference

Quality Aircraft Accessories. (n.d.). The Beginnings of the Bendix Magneto. Accessed June 16, 2019. https://www.qaa.com/blog/the-beginnings-of-the-bendix-magnetos

FINDING FUNDING AND OPPORTUNITY

There are numerous avenues to explore for funding for programs and events. These can range from competitive grants from local foundations or government agencies to funds from for-profit entities or local groups of enthusiasts. This section outlines some avenues for finding funding to support program activities.

Friends Groups

Most libraries have some type of support from a Friends group. If your library doesn't have a current Friends organization, consider helping to form one. The American Library Association (ALA) links to free toolkits for libraries of all types who are starting or working with Friends groups (http://www.ala.org/united/friends/orgtools). The power of Friends groups for assistance with funds shouldn't be underestimated. The Friends of the Seattle Public Library reported providing more than $56,000 in grants and other support to the Seattle Public Library in 2019 (Friends of the Seattle Public Library, 2020). The Tompkins County Friends of the Library group in Ithaca, New York, has biannual book sales to provide funding for library activities. They last reported giving the Tompkins County Public Library $335,000 from book sale proceeds in 2015–2016 (*Tompkins Weekly*, 2016). Funds received from Friends groups

CHAPTER 2

are often unrestricted, so they can be used for "above and beyond" activities that are not covered in the regular budget for programs and/or for provision of resources that might otherwise be restricted, as with federal grant funds, which often do not allow for buying some types of refreshments for programs. Similar to Friends groups, sometimes foundations are created explicitly to fund library activities and programs (see, for instance, https://www.signalmountainlibrary.com/index.php/about/mountain-library-foundation).

Family Foundations and Agencies: Local, Regional, and State

It is likely there are local or regional family foundations that support library efforts in your geographic or regional area. For example, the Tocker Foundation supports public libraries across rural Texas (those that serve populations of 12,000 or less); since 2006 it has given $12.5 million to 350 libraries in the state (Tocker Foundation, n.d.). The Langeloth Foundation in New York City, whose mission includes extending "availability of programs that promote healing to underserved populations" provided grant funding for the public library in Glens Falls, New York, to establish a consumer health information center and health programming (Foundation Directory Online, n.d.; Flaherty, 2013). Often foundations will require that organizations submit a letter of inquiry (LOI) before applying for a grant. This ensures that project goals align with the funder's expectations and cuts down on applications that don't fit the mission or funding requirements.

Another example of a regional opportunity is the Nord Family Foundation, whose purpose is to promote nonprofits in and around Loraine County, Ohio. Some funding mechanisms are based on other geographic criteria, such as the Catskill Watershed Corporation (CWC), which partners with the New York City Department of Environmental Protection to provide grants for educational programs in libraries, museums, schools, nonprofits, and vocational institutions on New York City's unique water supply. A simple internet search, limiting by region, will help to identify funders in your area.

Historical organizations are another rich possibility for support with programs, sometimes through funding and partnerships but also by providing speakers for historical talks and special events. Local history buffs are often involved in genealogy as well, which is another popular topic for programs in libraries of all types.

FUNDING

Government Support: Federal, State, and Local Agencies

There are a variety of agencies at all levels of government that support library and educational activities and programs. At the federal level, these include the National Endowment for the Arts (NEA), which sponsors initiatives such as the NEA's annual Big Read Program. More than $1 million in funding (average ranging from $5,000 to $15,000) was provided to seventy-nine organizations throughout the country for book discussions and events (National Endowment for the Arts, 2018). The National Endowment for the Humanities (NEH) supports libraries as well. In April 2019, the Hartford (Michigan) Public Library received $400,000 from the NEH to move to a new space (National Endowment for the Humanities, 2019). The NEH supports all types of humanities initiatives in a variety of educational settings.

The Library of Congress Center for the Book is another federally sponsored project that promotes books and libraries; its programs include series, events, lectures, partnerships, contests, and awards and prizes. Its website (http://read.gov) provides numerous resources that could be easily used to inspire and augment programs.

The Network of the National Library of Medicine, overseen by the National Library of Medicine, has eight network offices throughout the country. Often these regional offices offer small grants that can be used for programs related to health promotion. Some examples of recently funded programs include: Adulting 101, Collaborate and Educate: A School-Based Prescription Opioids Awareness Program, and Emerging Trends: Medical Data and Me Community Awareness Project (Network of the National Library of Medicine, n.d.).

State humanities councils, state and local arts councils, and state libraries are additional venues for program funding. State library agencies often administer federal funds, such as the Library Services and Technology Act (LSTA) funding from the Institute of Museum and Library Services (IMLS). For instance, the California state librarian administers LSTA grant funds for the Library Innovation Lab project (California Humanities, n.d.) through a competitive application process. The New York State Council on the Arts provides funding for programs and special projects through its Decentralization Grant Program, which is then administered through local arts councils. For example, the Roxbury Arts Group (RAG) in Margaretville, New York, is the administrator for the program in Delaware County and responsible for soliciting applications, choosing programs, and disbursing funding. There is a simple application process, and the Decentralization Grant Program through RAG has boosted summer programming offerings for public libraries in the region for years. Another easy program option is to invite local artists and authors, who are often willing to display their work, to participate in speakers' series and workshops for patrons.

Opportunities in Universities and Colleges

In university settings, there are often lecture series funds available for programs as well as events planning and coordination committees to assist with logistics. Other program funding may be available through the provost's, chancellor's, or president's office. Faculty from departments such as African American studies, art, communication, history, humanities, journalism, literature, and women's studies are also likely candidates to invite to present their work. Cooperative extension agencies, which are associated with land-grant universities, are another resource for program speakers on topics such as the environment, sustainable development, health, and nutrition.

An event can be centered on showcasing the library's collection. In April 2019, the University of North Carolina at Chapel Hill's Wilson Special Collections Library hosted an evening special event to share the library's recent acquisitions. The two-and-a-half-hour open house reception highlighted more than one hundred recent additions to the collection. Items such as a miniature Renaissance manuscript were on display, and library staff were available to guide patrons in an "up-close experience with rare and one-of-a-kind items from the North Carolina Collection, Rare Book Collection, Southern Folklife Collection, Southern Historical Collection and University Archives" (University of North Carolina, 2019). The relatively low-cost event brought dozens of visitors to the library, fostered a sense of community, and educated users about the vast array of unique resources available at the library.

At community colleges, there are often advisory boards, educational foundations, and/or grants and contracts departments that can assist with identifying and applying for program funding.

Service Organizations

Service groups such as Kiwanis International, Lions Club International, Rotary International, and Ruritan National are often enthusiastic supporters of libraries and may offer funding for library programs. The American Red Cross is another possible resource, offering program opportunities such as CPR training, disaster preparedness, and babysitting workshops at a low-cost.

FUNDING

For-Profit Sources

Local businesses are another resource for program funding. Organizations such as banks and credit unions; book, computer, department, hardware, and sporting goods stores; newspapers and utility companies; auto dealerships; and supermarkets have all been known to support their community libraries. Some national chains have foundation arms that offer dedicated grant funding to libraries, such as the Dollar General Literacy Foundation.

Other Local Resources

There are many low-cost or no-cost options for program opportunities, especially for one-off events that arise and present easy program ideas. For instance, when the last book in the Harry Potter series was published, public libraries around the world held celebrations that ranged from costume galas to all-night readings.

Consider inviting local experts in your area for program opportunities. For example, I was working at a public library when the novel *The DaVinci Code* was published. There was some controversy about its subject matter, and a number of patrons questioned whether it should be in the library's collection (even though the number of requests and holds for the book was extremely high). We responded by inviting a panel of local clergy to discuss the book at a library program. The ministers from the local Baptist and Methodist churches joined the local Catholic priest and Unitarian Universalist minister for a lively, well-attended discussion. After the program, there were no more questions about whether to retain the book in the collection or not.

Other local experts might include nutritionists or healthcare providers, real estate agents, legal aid lawyers, master gardeners, film buffs, collectors, authors, bike repair specialists, and filmmakers. The textbox that follows describes a series of programs undertaken with grant funding from a regional development organization, the Catskill Watershed Corporation.

PROGRAMMING IN ACTION: CATSKILL WATERSHED CORPORATION FUNDING FOR PUBLIC LIBRARY PROGRAMS

While I was the director of the Sidney Memorial Public Library, we successfully applied for an educational grant from a local development corporation that was established to protect water quality in the New

York City watershed west of the Hudson River, the Catskill Watershed Corporation. The grant provided for three programs: one for children and two for adults. The first was a production by the Arm of the Sea Theatre (located in the Hudson Valley, New York), a visual storytelling puppet and masque troupe whose mission is to combine art, ecology, and social action. The summertime program transformed the community room into a theatre stage with 12-foot puppets; it was attended by all ages, though the majority were middle schoolers. In order to gauge the educational impact of the program, we used short pre- and post-test surveys with questions on individuals' understanding of the watershed and water usage. Knowledge increased significantly according to the post-test results. The second sponsored program was a talk by a local documentarian, Nancy Burnett, who spoke about her oral history project "Behind the Scenes: The Inside Story of the Watershed Agreement"; the third was a panel of experts who presented on the creation of the CWC, which supplies New York City with what has been referred to as "the champagne of drinking water" and "an immaculate water supply" (Hu, 2018).

According to the New York State Department of Environmental Conservation (2020), the New York City Watershed is the largest unfiltered water supply in the United States, and provides nearly half of the state's population with drinking water (about 1.2 billion gallons daily). Given the village of Sidney and neighboring towns are adjacent to this important resource, the series of educational programs was enthusiastically supported and well attended.

REFERENCES

Hu, Winnie. (2018, January 18). "A Billion-Dollar Investment in New York's Water." *New York Times*. Accessed January 20, 2020. https://www.nytimes.com/2018/01/18/nyregion/new-york-city-water-filtration.html
New York State Department of Environmental Conservation. (2020). "Facts about the NYC Watershed." Accessed January 20, 2020. https://www.dec.ny.gov/lands/25599.html

RECAP

This chapter discussed different options for funding approaches and for finding additional resources to offer programs and host events. From dedicated funding to grants to gifts, libraries can take advantage of a wide variety of options to augment program opportunities. To be successful, programs don't need vast amounts of funds; the keys often lie in a bit of creativity and responsiveness to the user community.

REFERENCES

California Humanities. (n.d.). "Funding Opportunities." Accessed June 18, 2019. https://calhum.org/funding-opportunities/library-innovation-lab/

Flaherty, M. G. (2013). *The Public Library as Health Information Resource?* [dissertation] Syracuse University. http://surface.syr.edu/cgi/viewcontent.cgi?article=1081&context=it_etd

Foundation Directory Online (n.d.). "The Jacob and Valeria Langeloth Foundation." Accessed June 6, 2019. https://fconline.foundationcenter.org/fdo-grantmaker-profile/?key=LANG003

Friends of the Seattle Public Library. (2020). "How Funds Were Raised and Spent." Accessed December 14, 2020. https://www.friendsofspl.org/wp-content/uploads/2020/10/7.FinancialGraphic.png

National Endowment for the Arts. (2018, June 5). "National Endowment for the Arts Announces 2018-2019 NEA Big Read Grants." Accessed June 18, 2019. https://www.arts.gov/about/news/2018/national-endowment-arts-announces-2018-2019-nea-big-read-grants

National Endowment for the Humanities. (2019, April 4). "Hartford Public Library Gets $400,000 Grant." Accessed June 17, 2019. https://www.neh.gov/news/hartford-public-library-gets-400000-grant.

National Institutes of Health, Office of Management Acquisition and Policy. (2019). "Indirect Cost Definition and Example." Accessed June 14, 2019. https://oamp.od.nih.gov/dfas/indirect-cost-branch/indirect-cost-submission/indirect-cost-definition-and-example

Network of the National Library of Medicine. (n.d.). "Past Funded Projects." Accessed June 18, 2019. https://nnlm.gov/funding/funded

Tocker Foundation. (n.d.). "Supporting Public Libraries All across Rural Texas." Accessed June 17, 2019. https://tocker.org/

Tompkins Weekly. (2016, October 3). "Friends of the Library Booksale Starting This Weekend." Accessed December 14, 2020. https://www.tompkinsweekly.com/articles/friends-of-the-library-book-sale-starting-this-weekend/

United States Embassy, Burkina Faso. (2017, April 26). "The American Library Discusses Climate Change with Students." Accessed June 14, 2019. https://bf.usembassy.gov/american-library-discusses-climate-change-students/

University of North Carolina, University Libraries. (2019). "Recent Acquisitions Evening at the Wilson Special Collections Library." Accessed June 1, 2019. https://calendar.lib.unc.edu/event/5014070

3

MARKETING AND PUBLICIZING EVENTS

While many library staff are extremely talented and adept at providing an array of opportunities for their users, if patrons aren't aware of those opportunities, it is likely this lack of awareness will be reflected in event attendance levels.

Marketing is defined as "the process of determining the user communities' wants and needs, developing the products and services in response, and encouraging users (i.e., consumers) and potential users to make use of the products and services.... Regardless of library type, understanding the library's users, governing and funding bodies, community leaders, and administrators, and consulting with these groups are essential responsibilities of librarians" (Johnson, 2009, p. 192). Though she is discussing marketing in terms of collection development, Johnson's observations apply to all types of library services, including event and program planning.

This chapter discusses creating a marketing plan and marketing strategies, possible vectors of communication for publicizing events, and getting the word out at minimal cost. It also includes a number of examples of successful library events in a variety of library settings.

CRAFTING THE PLAN

As with any type of activity, a plan helps provide a framework and streamlines the process. The marketing plan functions to provide planned publicity. As such, it should include and be attentive to the organization's mission statement. Goals and objectives are common ways to frame a plan; they define what it is

CHAPTER 3

that you want to achieve and have the advantage of inculcating a method for measuring success. Methods of outreach should be addressed, and a timeline that outlines promotional activities for the coming year should be created as well. Other considerations are budgeting and staffing. Successful marketing plans are inclusive of all library efforts and often launch or highlight a slogan, brand, and/or logo. They should have clear rubrics for measurement (i.e., total attendance of events, numbers of new visitors, numbers of new followers, etc.). Evaluation and data measurement are discussed in more depth in chapter 4. The "Further Resources" section at the end of this chapter also includes suggestions for tools to assist with marketing.

Though marketing has largely been discussed and used in commercial or business domains, library staff have been using and adapting these strategies to positive effect; in this way, marketing strategies are used to determine how your library fits into the larger community. Librarians already use marketing tools such as identifying market segments through geographic (local, regional, national, international) and demographic (race, age, gender, socioeconomic status, employment status, education, ability) variables. Other variables include psychographic (lifestyles, opinions, attitudes) and product use (which product or resource is used, reasons why they're used; Demby, 2018).

Marketing strategies have four key elements, referred to as the four P's of the "marketing mix": product, place, price, and promotion (Demby, 2018). If we adapt Demby's elements to the library milieu, product equates to resources and services. Place involves getting those resources to patrons; this can be within the library or through outreach programs. Evaluating price involves looking at the cost, determining patron expectations, and meeting organizational goals. Promotion is letting your patrons know about the service, program, or event, and encouraging them to attend.

Questions that can guide the implementation of a marketing strategy include:

- What specific activities will be undertaken?
- When will these activities take place?
- How will these activities be completed?
- Who's responsible for completing these activities?
- How will the activities be monitored?
- What is the cost of these activities? (Demby, 2018)

For those organizations with funds for promotion and marketing, resources such as VerticalResponse, HubSpot, and Marketo may be employed. Often these companies have a free trial period to explore whether their services are appropriate for your organization. Guerilla marketing, a relatively new and unconventional approach, uses surprise and leverages energy and imagination rather than funds; the term was coined by Jay Conrad Levinson in his 1984 book, *Guerilla Marketing*. This style of marketing targets consumers in unexpected venues and involves creating a unique, thought-provoking campaign that evokes interest, generates "buzz," and sometimes becomes viral (Demby, 2018). Examples include outdoor (e.g., temporary artwork on sidewalks), indoor (e.g., temporary artwork in train stations or campus buildings), and experiential (e.g., executed in a manner that involves the public) approaches (Zantal-Wiener, 2018). No matter the approach, the next steps involve selecting what medium (or combination thereof, depending on your goals) to use, such as web/online, print and print ads, radio and TV, networking, and public venues.

GETTING THE WORD OUT: VECTORS OF COMMUNICATION

An easy way to advertise your events is to use a variety of communication channels, such as:

- Library's home resources, including:
  - Webpage
  - Facebook account
  - Twitter feed
  - Newsletter
- Fliers
  - Target to specific audience
  - Include in items that are checked out
  - Post beyond the library walls
- Library staff
  - Ensure they are aware of library events and programs
  - Ask them to spread the word in their communities
- Local news outlets
  - Create a media contact list if you don't already have one
  - Craft and circulate short press releases
    - include what, where, when, and cost (if there is any)
  - Include student newspapers and organizational communications (i.e., newsletters)

CHAPTER 3

- Sponsor or host an activity to highlight your program
  - Host an open house to highlight a community member's interest or research or the work of a community group, etc. (e.g., local birdwatchers' group; this could be coupled with birdhouse building workshop and/or citizen science lecture)
  - Sponsor a photo contest that is shared via social media; consider a small incentive to first five to ten attendees who share a photo from your program
  - Sponsor a craft workshop that includes making buttons that promote the event; consider including complementary topics as story time features

Regularly check in with patrons to learn where they heard about an event to monitor which methods are reaching them and which methods they are using to learn about library events. There are myriad alternative means, such as local parades, county fairs, and street markets—anywhere community members congregate—that can provide a communication forum. Consider getting patrons in on the act, with slogans such as, "Tell a friend about XYZ event," "Friends don't let friends miss a library event," or "Friends don't let friends attend a library event alone." Better yet: have patrons come up with the slogans to spread.

Reaching audiences who might not be regular library users has been a longtime challenge for library staff in all types of settings. Even in this digital era, getting out in the community and meeting folks where they are can help: fliers in barber shops, nail salons, markets, churches, and clubs (all with permission, of course) have been shown to be effective methods of attracting new patrons. Some libraries are fortunate enough to have fully staffed and funded marketing or public relations departments, yet the majority of libraries are more likely to depend on programming staff and regular communication channels to get the word out. Figure 3.1 depicts components of a promotion campaign.

Examples of Successful Promotion Programs

There are countless examples of successful promotion campaigns in the library milieu. Elsevier Publishing trademarked the slogan, "Never underestimate the importance of a librarian" in a popular promotional campaign. The American Library Association's trademark "@ your library," first registered in 2003, still resonates and is widely used today. Libraries of all types can download and use the logo free of charge, as long as they adhere to the ALA's guidelines for use.

MARKETING AND PUBLICIZING EVENTS

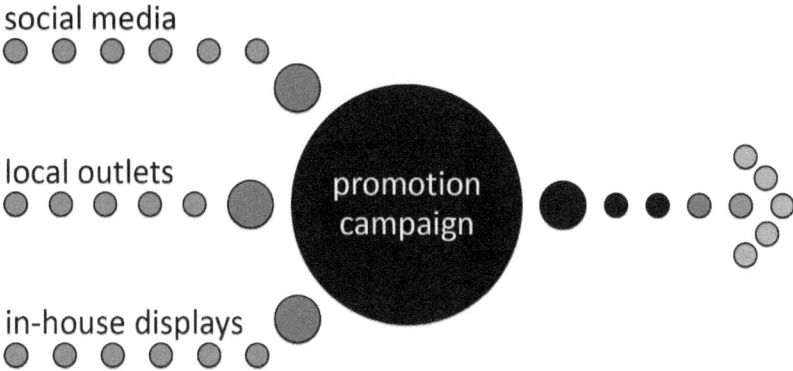

Figure 3.1. Promotion campaign components. *Courtesy of the author*

For more information, see https://www.ala.org/ala/pio/campaign/downloadlogos/yourlibrary.htm.

The Troy (Michigan) Public Library provides an inspired example of a well-thought-out campaign to promote awareness of its budget woes. The library used a social media hoax to stage a book burning party in order to bring attention to looming opposition to the library budget. For a video summary of the successful project, see https://vimeo.com/35758683.

Promotion can take on different meanings in different library settings. For instance, in the healthcare arena, offering incentives can work to entice busy clinicians to take advantage of opportunities and events they might not otherwise attend. Library workshops that provide continuing education credits are a sure-fire way to appeal to busy practitioners. In the case described below, because of careful planning with key players and incentives such as continuing education credits and a free lunch, a series of simple e-mails and one-on-one communication was all the promotion that was needed to dramatically increase attendance, as detailed by Erica Brody.

PROGRAMMING IN ACTION: CONTINUING EDUCATION EVENT FOR SCHOOL OF DENTISTRY FACULTY

Challenge: Providing information literacy and research training to School of Dentistry Faculty

- Most School of Dentistry faculty are clinicians who have limited experience conducting research, which is not required for the DDS degree.

- Dental school faculty have significant teaching and clinical responsibilities, therefore:
  - They have little time for research or learning how to conduct research.
  - Scheduling a continuing education event is difficult.

History: The previous library programs on consumer oral health information and predatory publishing were conducted with eight or fewer professors in attendance.

Planning for Fall Semester program:

- Topic selection: The liaison librarian identified several topics for consideration and vetted them with two key thought leaders at the school, the senior associate dean and a faculty member who is good at thinking about the needs of the whole school rather than just his department. They recommended teaching about systematic reviews.
- Scheduling: The liaison librarian consulted with top administrators familiar with class and clinic schedules to identify a time that would be convenient for the greatest number of faculty.
- Location: The program was held in a classroom at the School of Dentistry so faculty could remain in the building, adding to the convenience of attending.
- Incentives: The senior associate dean of the School of Dentistry offered funds to provide attendees with lunch, allowing them to focus on the program during their lunch hour. In addition, attendees earned continuing dental education credit paid for and coordinated by the Continuing Education Department at the School of Dentistry.
- Promotion: The librarian mentioned the program during meetings and consultations with dental faculty. An e-mail was sent out three weeks before the program and a few days before the program to recruit participants.

Evaluation:
- Eighteen faculty members attended the event, 100 percent more than previous events.
- Participants asked questions throughout the program, indicating engagement with the material.
- Eight attendees completed evaluations of the program:
  - 100 percent indicated they were satisfied with the event and that the teaching methods were excellent.
  - Comments included:
    - "Very awesome lecture. I learned a lot and [the librarian] was very thorough."

☐ "Excellent overview of systematic reviews and EBD."
☐ "Good course."
☐ "Excellent presentation, with valuable advice for reviewing literature and preparing a paper."
☐ "Excellent. I loved the process layout organized on the slides. It made everything approachable and less intimidating."

Erica Brody, MSLS, MPH
Research and Education Librarian, Liaison to School of Dentistry
Tompkins-McCaw Library
Virginia Commonwealth University
Richmond, Virginia

ESTABLISHING AN ONGOING MARKETING PROGRAM

Once mechanisms for marketing are in place (e.g., regular Twitter feed, bulletin boards in local venues) endeavor to ensure there is a dedicated staff member responsible for promotional activities. In libraries with smaller staffing levels, consider adding the duty to a willing candidate's job description. Outside of the immediate staff, Friends group members, board members, student interns, and oversight committee members can serve not only as advocates but also as conduits for helping to promote events and programs through their channels and networks. A creative way to approach promotion, "gamification," is described below by Dr. Noah Lenstra.

PROGRAMMING IN ACTION: GAMIFYING LIBRARY PROMOTION

Are you seeking to build your library audience and attract new people to your programs? Consider adopting an approach that has worked well for everyone from Pokemon® Go to the Nike®+ Run Club: gamification! Briefly, gamification consists of adding typical elements of game play (e.g., point scoring, competition with others, rules of play) to marketing in order to encourage engagement with a product or service. Libraries have been doing gamification for a while, often without even realizing it. Here are highlights of some examples to get your creative juices flowing.

CHAPTER 3

In September 2019, the Pierce County Library System in Washington State invited its community to "get ready to pick up a book, shoot some hoops, and even have a pillow fight." The library's "Community Adventure features a game board and activities to help families connect with each other and their community while learning and earning prizes." In a press release, Pierce County Library's executive director Georgia Lomax said, "Opportunities to learn are all around us. Our Community Adventure gives parents a fun guide to become more aware of those learning opportunities. With hands on, eyes open and feet walking, this new service tours families through their community, while learning and having fun" (Pierce County Library System, 2019).

These types of gamified programs can also be done through partnerships. Where I live in North Carolina, the North Carolina Arboretum has teamed up with public libraries for the past five years on an initiative called ecoEXPLORE. Participants sign up at the library and "play" by taking pictures of the natural world around them. They earn points and badges for documenting different facets of the natural world and can earn prizes (provided by the Arboretum) that they pick up at the library. To take this initiative to the next level, some libraries have installed butterfly gardens, started checking out nature exploration backpacks, and hosted programs on everything from ornithology to backyard gardening.

Meanwhile, in New York State, three mostly rural library systems teamed up with the Network of the National Library of Medicine to launch the Library Moon Walk challenge in early spring 2019 to build up interest and enthusiasm for the 2019 Collaborative Summer Library Program, which focused on outer space. The libraries built a website (https://librarymoon walk.sals.edu/) that challenges community members to be active however they wish—walking, bicycling, rolling, yoga, whatever works!—and to collectively walk together to the moon. The website also includes a link to health programming offered by the three library systems.

In Akron, Ohio, the library's "summer program rewards reading and movement" (Freeman, 2019). The library's Mind, Body & Sole reading/exercise log encourages people to keep track of both what they read and how they exercise. Both are rewarded and incentivized through fun programs throughout the summer.

Gamification can occur over extended periods of time, but it can also be used for specific programs. In the small town of Crandon in Northern Wisconsin, the library teamed up with a slew of local partners, including the school district and the public health department, to offer a Healthy Foods Competition to challenge families to see who could make the tastiest dishes using healthy foods. OCLC/Webjunction profiled the library as part of its Health Happens at the Library initiative (Morris, 2015).

As these examples show, gamification can be used to promote and encourage participation in library programs in all kinds of different ways.

A few common tendencies include the creative use of technology and community partnerships. Think about gamifying your library by reaching out to others and trying something new with technology. Ancillary positive effects will include strengthened relationships with potential programming partners and increased technical capacity in your library. Let's play!

References

Freeman, L. (2019, May 29). "Summer Program Rewards Reading and Movement." *Record-Courier*. Accessed December 14, 2020. https://www.record-courier.com/news/20190529/summer-program-rewards-reading-and-movement

Morris, L. (2015, September 16). "Healthy Foods Competition Heats Up at Crandon Public Library." *WebJunction*. Accessed December 4, 2020. https://www.webjunction.org/news/webjunction/healthy-foods-competition-heats-up-at-crandon-public-library.html

Pierce County Library System. (2019, September 11). "Community Scavenger Hunt for Young Children, a New Library Learning Service." Accessed December 14, 2020. https://www.piercecountylibrary.org/files/library/ourcommunityadventure092019-final.pdf

Noah Lenstra, PhD, MSLS
Assistant Professor of Library and Information Science
Director of Let's Move in Libraries
University of North Carolina Greensboro

With some interactive programs, the activity itself has so much appeal that promotion can be as simple as making an announcement once it has been established. An example is the ever-popular therapy dogs visit at academic libraries, particularly during stressful times of the year, such as finals. Leila Ledbetter provides a description of such a program at Duke University in the textbox that follows.

PROGRAMMING IN ACTION: THERAPY DOGS AT THE DUKE UNIVERSITY MEDICAL CENTER LIBRARY

Getting Started

Organizational Buy-in for Bringing Therapy Dogs to the Library

Be prepared to answer questions from management about insurance, protecting patrons, providing staff time, cleanup, and parking provision.

CHAPTER 3

Finding the Right Therapy Dog Organization to Work With

Not all therapy dog organizations are created equal. Make sure you talk to a couple of different groups and find out what they will require from the library in terms of space, how much lead time they need for an event, and anything else they might like you to provide. Also investigate other institutions they have worked with and contact those organizations to see if they can provide a reference or offer any advice about working with that particular therapy dog group.

We suggest scheduling two to three dogs for each hour to hour and a half of the event. The organization will have suggestions for this. Frequently, one or two dog/handler teams do not show up, so plan accordingly.

Choosing a Location for the Event

Pick a location that is easy to direct people to but is either out of the main flow of patron traffic or enclosed in some way. Some patrons prefer not to interact with the dogs, and they need to be able to conduct their business at the library without concern.

Allow for lots of floor space—people will be getting down on the floor to interact with and pet the dogs. Allow for at least ten feet between each team. This allows the dogs their space, gives handlers room for any equipment they might bring, and leaves room for visitors to gather around the dogs.

Marketing

Put fliers and posters up and send promotional messages out to patron groups two to three weeks before, one week before, and on the day of the event.

On the day of the event, place posters up at all the entrances to the building. If you have a lot of foot traffic by your building, you may want to put signage up outside as well to attract as many attendees at possible and to draw people in.

Providing for the Dogs and Handlers

Things to provide beforehand:

1. Details about the facility and the location where the event will be held.
2. Let the organization know if there is a particular event you're having them in for. For instance, sometimes the handlers will dress their

dogs for particular occasions, and this gives them something to engage with the visitors about.
3. Map to your location with parking and with dog-friendly walking directions from where they are parked to where the event will be held. On the map, point out "potty" areas and the nearest trash can for proper waste disposal.
4. Provide the handlers with a last-minute contact number (preferably a mobile phone since you may be running around setting up) for a staff member who may be able to help them.

Day of the event:

1. Water bowl and water
2. Parking passes
3. Let the handlers know the policy for photography, as this can vary from library to library
4. Chairs for the handlers—some like to sit on the floor with their dogs and some prefer to sit in a chair

Providing for Visitors on the Day of the Event

Provide hand sanitizer and pet hair rollers for people's clothes. It is also useful to have towels or blankets people can put in their laps to protect their clothes from pet hair or in case someone is wearing shorts or a skirt.

Have a plan for getting people's permission for pictures. You might provide permission slips and those who prefer not to have their picture taken wear stickers that say, "Please no pictures," or have a sign up in the area that says patrons are agreeing to have their picture taken if they participate.

Cleanup

There is always a lot of hair! Inform your environmental services people that you will be having dogs in the building and that you may need a staff person available to help clean up after the event, or have them provide you with cleaning equipment.

Leila Ledbetter, MLIS, AHIP
Research and Education Librarian, Liaison to the School of Nursing
Duke University Medical Center Library

CHAPTER 3

Another way to respond to the user community is through events directed at providing a discrete service, such as absentee voter registration. At American University, an ongoing program was created after the success of an initial trial event. A description of that process by Dr. Gwendolyn Reece follows below.

PROGRAMMING IN ACTION: ABSENTEE BALLOT DAY

Absentee Voter Registration in an Academic Library

American University Library held its first Absentee Ballot Day on September 25, 2018. During this event, 1,005 students requested absentee ballots, enabling them to vote for officials running for office in their home jurisdictions. This event empowered our students to vote, positioned the library as an ally that empowers people to navigate government information for the purposes of civic engagement, strengthened our relationship with student government, and allowed us to introduce students to high-quality, nonpartisan information sources. In order to encourage and facilitate other libraries to offer similar events, I created a toolkit (https://subjectguides .library.american.edu/absentee_ballot_day) and a listserv to build community and share planning, which is still active. (To join the listserv, e-mail listserv@listserv.american.edu with a blank subject and type, "subscribe ABSENTEEBALLOTDAY-L [Your Name]."

Making the Case: Why Is Absentee Ballot Day a Good Idea?

To be healthy, representative democracies require an engaged and informed citizenry. We know that early voting behavior establishes patterns that shape voter behavior for the rest of their lives (Gerber, Green, & Shachar, 2003; Plutzer, 2002; Prior, 2010). For many of our students, the first time they are eligible to vote is when they are attending university.

However, our students face significant barriers to exercising their franchise. University students move frequently. If they register to vote at a temporary address, they must reregister with every move. Many on-campus voter registration drives register students at their temporary addresses, exacerbating this problem. Secondly, students are often more knowledgeable about and committed to local politics in their home district. If they are intending to return home after they leave university, then the decisions made at the state and local level at home will significantly impact their lives, and they should have a voice in those jurisdictions. Finally, for students temporarily living in the District of Columbia, such as students at American University, they would give up having a meaningful vote somewhere else if they were to register in Washington, DC, where we have no voting members in Congress.

There is thus a strong case for registering students to vote in their home jurisdictions—but this also presents challenges for students. Many students cannot realistically travel to vote, either because of distance or time away from school and/or work. Lower-income students are especially affected by these barriers. Most jurisdictions allow university students living away from home to vote absentee, but the process and paperwork for each jurisdiction varies widely and the difficulty in understanding and navigating the process is also variable. Some jurisdictions have emphasized removing barriers to voting and others have focused on erecting more. Furthermore, many younger students do not have experience with "snail mail" and do not know where to get stamps, have never addressed an envelope, and don't know where they should deposit the mail. Therefore, an Absentee Ballot Day event empowers students to vote.

Why Should It Be a Library Event?

Public libraries have long considered assisting people to be engaged citizens as a critical part of their mission. Academic libraries have historically focused their efforts on helping students succeed in their specific academic programs. With the increasing emphasis on lifelong learning, positioning the library as providing information literacy training for the purposes of engaged citizenry is an appropriate expansion of our core mission. Absentee Ballot Day allows the library to assist students in navigating government forms and processes and to promote high-quality, nonpartisan political information. Libraries also occupy a unique position in universities. We support everyone. One of my high-level goals is that I want our students to experience the library not as a static repository, but as an ally that empowers people through information—and I want them to carry this conception of libraries with them throughout their lives.

American University Library partnered with student government, which I strongly recommend. Our successful collaboration on this event set up a stronger relationship with student government, to our mutual benefit. While student governments often independently hold voter registration drives, our student government expressed immense gratitude to us for taking the lead on this initiative and then partnering with them. National Voter Registration Day is always set in the end of September and is the final date on which you can be sure you will meet every state's registration deadline. However, student government officers change each year, and their duties do not commence until the beginning of fall term. This makes a September event difficult for them to plan and execute. We did most of the planning over the summer and then brought the officers in when they returned to campus.

CHAPTER 3

Costs

The real costs of hosting an Absentee Ballot Day event are minimal. We supplied stamps, envelopes, and printing/copying. Marketing expenses included posters and "I Registered Absentee" stickers.

Who Needs to Be Involved in Planning?

Assign either a project lead or a small project leadership group. The members of this group need to understand the whole process and be empowered to make decisions. During the event itself, at least one project lead should be on-site throughout.

The library information technology staff will need to arrange the setup for computers and the printer/copier. If you are using a voting portal, such as Vote.org or TurboVote, set that as the homepage on each computer's browser.

Whoever is responsible for building management will need to plan the layout of the physical tables and stanchions. You will need an event site that can handle lines and noise.

Marketing the event will require a graphic designer, someone facile with social media, and someone who can write press releases. You will also want to coordinate with any partners on communication efforts.

Once they return to campus, include student government officers to help think through communication, marketing, and volunteer recruitment. Other partners can be included in the planning or a member of the planning group can coordinate the partners. Ensuring that all partners stay on message is critical. Draft invitations for partners and volunteers are included in the toolkit.

Planning

You will need to decide the following:

- Date: National Voter Registration Day (recommended)
- Times: We offered 8 a.m–10 p.m.
- What you will provide:
    - Stamps
    - Envelopes
    - Free printing
    - Free copying of IDs (we made two for each state that required it)
    - Consulting help with the forms
    - Gathering the envelopes and taking them to the post office
    - Signed witnesses

MARKETING AND PUBLICIZING EVENTS

- Promotion for information resources (we handed out Vote411.org cards from the League of Women Voters)
- Whether you will use a portal site, such as Vote.org or TurboVote, etc.
- Logistics setup
  - Laptop/desktop computers in a set area
  - Printer/copier
  - Line control
  - Whiteboard
    - We listed each state that required an ID
    - We kept track of other unusual things (states that needed signed witnesses or unusual information like precinct code, etc.)
  - Poster explaining how to address an envelope (an example is in the toolkit)
  - Wayfinding to the event location
- Whether you will provide assistance after they receive their ballot
  - Stamps
  - Signed witnesses
  - ID copying
- Partners
  - Student government (recommended)
  - I strongly suggest that groups be strictly nonpartisan
    - League of Women Voters
    - Alumni Association
- Volunteers
  - Instructions/agreements of nonpartisan purpose (draft in the toolkit)
  - Roles
    - Directing people to the event
    - Helping with the forms
    - Gathering/distributing print forms
    - Copying IDs
    - Distributing stamps and "I Registered Absentee" stickers, and providing any follow-up information (for us, Vote411 cards and instructions about ballot support)
  - Library employees
  - Student government volunteers
  - External organization volunteers (we had League of Women Voters and the Alumni Association)
- Marketing
  - Ask student government to promote the event through their communication channels
  - Signs
  - Social media
  - "I Registered Absentee" stickers

○ Contact the student paper and ask for an article in advance and to report on the event after the fact
• Student radio/TV—ask them to make regular announcements

Gwendolyn Reece, PhD, MS, MA
Director of Research, Teaching and Learning
American University
Washington, DC

References

Gerber, A. S., Green, D. P., & Shachar, R. (2003). "Voting May Be Habit-Forming: Evidence from a Randomized Field Experiment." *American Journal of Political Science, 47* (5), 540–50.
Plutzer, E. (2002). "Becoming a Habitual Voter: Inertia, Resources, and Growth in Young Adulthood." *American Political Science Review, 96*(1), 41–56.
Prior, M. (2010). "You've Either Got It or You Don't? The Stability of Political Interest over the Life Cycle." *Journal of Politics, 72*(3), 747–66. https://doi.org/10.1017/S0022381610000149.

In the final Programming in Action section in this chapter, Taylor Johnson describes "the art of the pivot," or how a program was adapted to respond to early challenges in the COVID-19 pandemic.

PROGRAMMING IN ACTION: THE ART OF THE PIVOT IN AN UNCERTAIN LANDSCAPE

Background

The North Carolina Library Association's STEM Librarianship in NC (NCLA STEM-LINC) section seeks to connect librarians with common interests in science, technology, engineering, and/or mathematics (STEM) to opportunities for education and professional development. STEM-LINC programming is rooted in quarterly events alternating with in-person gatherings (tours, training, etc.) in the spring and fall and virtual meetings (webinars) in the winter and summer. While planning for the spring 2020 in-person program started shortly after the winter webinar, progress ground to a halt in March when the state suddenly shut down and what would become the months-long isolation to fight the coronavirus pandemic began.

Pivot #1

The next steps were relatively obvious. STEM-LINC would flip the standard order and migrate the spring event to a webinar. But something else was happening. Possible speakers became harder to reach. Even the steadfast programming committee became slower to respond to e-mails as members scrambled to adjust to their work-from-home environments. Professional development became a giant question mark when the normally thriving summer library conference season saw cancellations and moves to virtual programming. The mental and emotional toll of this new era set in as the world learned this would be not merely a blip in daily operations but a complete lifestyle change.

It took a few weeks to develop routines while many explored online happy hours, virtual game nights, and other ways to avoid complete isolation. When talks surrounding a STEM-LINC virtual program resumed, the consensus was that one more webinar on anyone's calendar, whether a speaker or attendee, stood the risk of being lost in a sea of online training, Microsoft Teams meetings, and Zoom calls. Could there be a solution that did not involve a webcam and "We can't hear you; please unmute"?

Pivot #2

On April 22, 2020, society reached a significant landmark: the fiftieth Earth Day, signifying a half-century of efforts to clean and protect the world's natural resources. Organizations from government agencies to university departments had daylong, weeklong, and even yearlong plans to celebrate this milestone. Similarly, libraries had advertised events, but did all of this still happen? As everyone lost touch, the outcome was unknown. STEM-LINC, being an intermediary between libraries and environmental education, was well equipped to investigate and disseminate findings.

In fact, this question could become the leading topic of a series that would bring STEM activities and conversations relevant to librarianship to NCLA members across the state in a newsletter. A frenzy of surveys ensued: Did your library do anything for Earth Day, and can you share pictures? What should our newsletter be called? What else is going on in the world that you want to talk about? STEM-LINC was met with virtual crickets. Even two months into quarantine, members still lacked time to devote to professional development as uneven workloads and personal pivots consumed the day-to-day. Maybe, it was decided, the climate was not quite right for a newsletter.

Pivot #3

But what about the fiftieth Earth Day? A handful of surveyed members had confirmed their organizations still supported events in North Carolina.

CHAPTER 3

Could there be more to share? A brief search of Facebook, Google, and some of the state's leading environmental education organizations showed that, yes, North Carolinians still came together (virtually) to celebrate this landmark occasion!

Over the course of a weekend, since it was by this point early May and time to produce a spring program was dwindling, STEM-LINC semi-systematically searched social media sites and the web to compile a list of Earth Day events in North Carolina. The survey submissions were included as well as programs gleaned from other libraries and organizations. Thanks to technology, even some events that happened live were recorded and will be available for years to come. After some proofing, a thematic picture and header were added, and this improvised digital publication entitled "NC Celebrates the 50th Earth Day" was distributed across the NCLA listserv.

While the e-mail did not pack the punch of a speaker or provide the continuous informing power of a newsletter, it met a goal core to STEM-LINC's mission: "to provide an opportunity for . . . exchange of information in STEM librarianship." Not only that, it reassured recipients that there were still fun and engaging activities happening to excite the public about the importance of conservation, participating in nature-based activities, and being environmentally responsible. At the very least, the e-mail presented a pretty picture and a digestible list of links in overflowing inboxes bogged down with meeting invites and bad news.

Conclusion

Professional development can fall low on the list of priorities when the daily operations are uncertain or uneven, whether personally or because of a global pandemic. In order to fulfill its commitment, STEM-LINC had to adapt not once, not twice, but three times as leaders persevered instead of giving up. Maybe the Earth Day e-mail was not groundbreaking, but it found a way to bring value and uplifting information to members during a time of possible burnout and exhaustion. Most importantly, it showed that even in times of uncertainty, librarians can band together to accomplish goals, keep each other connected and informed through sharing information, and maybe bring a little blue sky to each other's day along the way.

Taylor Abernethy Johnson, MSLS
STEM-LINC Member-at-Large Representing Special Libraries
Assistant Director
US Environmental Protection Agency Library
UNC Contractor
Research Triangle Park, NC

STEM Librarianship in NC Website: https://nclaonline.org/stem-linc

Distributed List of Earth Day Activities

NC Celebrates the 50th Earth Day

Though Earth Day looked a little different this year, some organizations still commemorated the milestone with virtual programs and celebrations. Here are a few of NCLA STEM-LINC's favorites:

- NC DEQ reflected on 50 years of Earth Day in NC with their #NCEarthDay50 campaign including an Instagram photo challenge (https://www.instagram.com/p/B-2jD_sn-zr/?utm_source=ig_web_copy_link) and videos from environmental educators: https://deq.nc.gov/outreach-education/earth-day-2020
- NC Government & Heritage Library created a list of online NCPedia resources: https://statelibrary.ncdcr.gov/blog/2020/04/02/earth-day-2020-celebrate-north-carolina-state-parks-online
- NC Museum of Natural Sciences held Earth Week opportunities with online talks and activities: https://naturalsciences.org/calendar/news/earth-week-opportunities/
- The NC Zoo held Earth Week with a series of Facebook Live videos on gopher frogs, pollinator pods, and more: https://www.facebook.com/nczoo/posts/10157086226927327
- NC State's Sustainability Council and University Sustainability Office pivoted their big plans for Earth Day and held online events and challenges all month long (https://sustainability.ncsu.edu/get-involved/events/earth-day/) while the NC State annual Earth Fair went virtual for the first time ever: https://sustainability.ncsu.edu/earth-fair-2020/
- Wake Forest University's Special Collections and Archives published an online subject guide: https://zsr.wfu.edu/2020/celebrating-the-50th-anniversary-of-earth-day-resources-in-special-collections-archives/
- Forsyth County Public Library and Wake Forest University's Z. Smith Reynolds Library contributed to the Piedmont Environmental Alliance's Virtual Earth Day Fair: https://www.peanc.org/virtual-earth-day-fair
- Charlotte Mecklenburg Library promoted a collection of books on sustainability through their digital reading platform: https://www.facebook.com/cmlibrary/posts/10159514809889256
- Polk Library held an Earth Day Storytime: https://polklibrary.org/storytime/
- Duke Lemur Center hosted an all-day, virtual Earth Day Extravaganza: https://lemur.duke.edu/earth-day2020/
- Several scientists from the U.S. Environmental Protection Agency's RTP campus made STEM activity videos like this one: https://youtu.be/tx_K28tJKU0

CHAPTER 3

- Keep Durham Beautiful held a Virtual Earth Month where they shared educational webinars, crafts, and other online opportunities like the Eco-Art Competition: https://www.keepdurhambeautiful.org/eco-art-competition

RECAP

This chapter touched on marketing strategies and promotion of library events and provided tips for how to get the word out. The most effective and lowest cost promotional tool in the programming librarians' arsenal is word-of-mouth, whether that's through Instagram or in person. The wide array of examples of successful activities and approaches from a variety of practicing librarians and scholars demonstrated how the principles are operationalized in the library setting.

FURTHER RESOURCES

Cowan, A. (2013, April 16). "Twelve Fast and Inexpensive Ways to Market Your Library." *Library Connect*. Accessed January 2, 2020. https://libraryconnect.elsevier.com/articles/12-fast-and-inexpensive-ways-market-your-library

Dempsey, K. (n.d.). "How to Use Marketing in Your Library." Princh. Accessed January 2, 2020. https://princh.com/how-to-use-marketing-in-a-library-kathy-dempsey-interview/#.Xdr4wldKg2w

Ibach, M. (n.d.). *Library Marketing Plans*. South Central Library System, Madison, WI. Accessed January 2, 2020. https://www.scls.info/pr/toolkit

McClary, T. (2012, January 18). "How to Develop a Marketing Plan for Your Library." *New Jersey State Library Marketing Blog*. Accessed January 2, 2020. https://www.njstatelib.org/how_to_develop_a_marketing_plan_for_your_public/

New York Public Library. "Market Research." Accessed January 2, 2020. https://www.nypl.org/node/5722

Porter-Reynolds, D. (2014). *Streamlining Library Programming: How to Improve Services and Cut Costs*. Santa Barbara, CA: Libraries Unlimited.

Potter, N. (2012). *The Library Marketing Toolkit*. London, UK: Facet Publishing.

Wichman, E. T. (2012). *Librarian's Guide to Passive Programming*. Santa Barbara, CA: Libraries Unlimited.

Marketing associations are an excellent resource for recent publications of marketing research: American Marketing Association (https://www.ama.org), Direct Marketing

Association (https://thedma.org); Insights Association (https://www.insightsassociation.org).

REFERENCES

Demby, P. (2018). *Developing Your Marketing Plan*. New York StartUP! Marketing Plan Workshop #2. New York Public Library. Accessed January 2, 2020. https://www.nypl.org/sites/default/files/2018_new_york_startup_marketing_plan_workshop.pdf

Johnson, P. (2009). *Fundamentals of Collection Development and Management* (2nd ed.). Chicago: American Library Association.

Zantal-Wiener, A. (2018, July 30). "What Is Guerilla Marketing? 7 Examples to Inspire Your Brand." HubSpot. Accessed January 2, 2020. https://blog.hubspot.com/marketing/guerilla-marketing-examples

4

EVALUATION AND OUTCOME MEASURES

Generally speaking, the societal value of libraries is largely taken for granted. Thus, historically the need to prove their worth hasn't been as intense as for other entities in an institution or town, such as a safety inspection bureau or a recreation center. There are likely many reasons for this. Almost everywhere, there exists an ardent and vocal community of library users who will advocate on their libraries' behalf. There have been large research projects spanning multiple states showing that, for example, good libraries in public schools increase scholastic performance (Lance & Kachel, 2018) or that public libraries increase property values (Barron et al., 2005; Diamond et al., 2010).

Because many of the benefits that libraries provide take years to manifest, it's not logical that one library on a local level would be asked to justify a specific service, such as children's story hour or the existence of a historical archive. This combination of enthusiastic advocates, broad evidence of widely appreciated benefits, and organizational competence has sheltered libraries somewhat from some of the brutal scrutiny that often arises during periods of financial shortfall. Moreover, many public services (e.g., safety inspection offices, garbage collection, prison operation) can be done by businesses that advocate privatizing that service; mercifully, there is little for-profit competition to create historical archives or libraries.

While libraries may tend to have less pressure than similar-sized services to justify their existence, that's not the main reason for evaluations, in general. The main reason evaluations are performed in education and medicine and fire departments is to examine and improve the quality of services. Admittedly, for one hundred libraries, improving quality is going to mean one hundred different

CHAPTER 4

things. But in this era where information is increasingly digital, where the internet is flooded with questionable information, and where libraries are expected to do many new things for their communities, the need to evaluate has become more important than ever before. This chapter will attempt to lay out in simple terms a process by which librarians can articulate their goals (on the event, service, or institution level), make those goals measurable, and assess whether the library is achieving them.

MAKING AN EVALUATION PLAN

As with countless library activities, an evaluation plan or process is necessary to measure the effectiveness of your efforts with regard to some specific goal, be it on the level of a summer reading program or a community health objective. The evaluation process should be considered and agreed upon during the planning stages and tied to goals and objectives, so that you're ready to collect data before, during, and after the event is launched. Thus, step one in an evaluation process is always assessing and agreeing upon your goal(s).

Goals work best when they are agreed to by the key players involved. Before getting bogged down in the science of evaluations and what will be measured, it is profoundly useful to have widely agreed-upon objectives. Often these start out very vague, such as: We want more young adults using and feeling welcome in the library. Does using the library only for internet access count as using the library? What does "feeling welcome" mean? Any goal can be turned into measurable objectives—admittedly, some more easily than others—but starting with everyone on the same general page is an important first step toward success. Once you know what your basic goal is, the next step is to translate that goal into measurable objectives.

In common parlance, the words "goals" and "objectives" are often used synonymously. Among evaluation specialists, objectives are more often described as measureable or tangible things that reflect the spirit and intent of goals or that are linked to a goal. In the example above, aspiring to have young people feel more welcome at a public library, having a record of the number of visits by young people or the number of books and downloads borrowed by young people over time would provide logical indicators of that objective. It may be difficult to capture attendance; consider, though, that if most of the youth and few of the adults in your community use bicycles for transport, keeping track of the number of bicycles in the library's bike rack could be an indirect indicator of young adults' library use. Hence, use of bike rack data may become one of the inputs for monitoring the objective.

In the education and health communities, the acronym SMART is used to characterize ideal objectives. SMART objectives are:

- *Specific:* They are clear and precise and relatively objective.
- *Measurable:* It is easy to count, measure, objectively identify these events.
- *Achievable:* These are doable elements that are likely to occur if your goals are being achieved. Rare events (e.g., an attendee afterward won a full-tuition scholarship to university) that are hard to attain are not appropriate.
- *Realistic:* It is highly plausible that this can happen.
- *Timely:* It will happen and be recordable in the period of evaluation.

There are many tools available to aid in creating SMART objectives. For guidance and a simple checklist to aid in the development of SMART indicators, the Chartered Management Institute provides an easy starting place at https://www.managers.org.uk/~/media/Files/Campus CMI/Checklists PDP/Setting SMART objectives.ashx.

It's common that as goals are fine-tuned and translated into objectives with SMART indicators, many measures will be considered and rejected and you will end up with some combination or collection of indicators to assess your objective. In the example above, the goal was "We want more young adults using and feeling welcome in the library." We determined that as programs unfold, in order to be more inclusive to young adults, (1) we can monitor the number of borrowed items by young adults and (2) it may be difficult to monitor how many come into the library, but (3) we can monitor bikes in the bike rack which may be an indirect indicator of attendance. But these together actually capture nothing about "feeling welcome." Thus, while indicators 1 and 3 are SMART and may capture indications that more young adults are using the library, they do not capture all aspects of the widely agreed-upon goal, and together they are an inadequate measurement for this goal. Somehow an indicator of "feeling more welcome" needs to be added.

Classically, once the goals are understood, the selection of indicators for assessing and articulating your objectives involves an assessment of what data are available and what kinds of assessments or interviews or monitoring is possible in your setting. What data have been collected already? Will different stakeholders be interested in different indicators and/or combinations of indicators? When one presents this information to stakeholders, what will be more compelling for them?

CHAPTER 4

- Will it be attendance numbers?
  - Will it be new users?
  - Will it be a targeted demographic that has thus far been underserved (e.g. homeless teens)?
- Will it be evidence of (new) skill acquisition by attendees?
- Will it be successful fundraising efforts?
- Will it be higher visibility for the library?
- Will it be ratings of attendees' satisfaction?

These are just a few considerations of types of information that can guide the evaluation process, and of course each may have different approaches and requirements for data collection. For example, attendance numbers and fundraising counts are rather straightforward data points and regularly captured and reported in many places. Evidence of skill acquisition or user satisfaction or increased library visibility may take more effort and avenues to determine how to quantify and analyze, however. This may not be doable within the comfort level of your team. The chapter continues with a discussion of types of data to collect and approaches for collecting and analyzing data, including some tools that can help with the process.

DATA COLLECTION

As stated above, collection of your desired indicators for evaluation will be guided by the program goals and objectives that were determined during the planning phase. Goals attend to broad organizational considerations and, as used here, objectives describe the specific desired result that will help articulate that goal. Many events in a library are done for stimulation, celebration, or entertainment purposes. In general, attendance is the classic indicator of the worth of an event. But some programs are designed to induce specific outcomes, such as helping people register for Medicare or to reduce their home's risk of wildfire damage. Programs designed to induce outcomes are important to evaluate, with the outcomes sought being the ideal measurement of the impact or end result. Such programs require a follow-up process to assess whether attendees achieved their objectives. Table 4.1 includes examples of basic ways to measure different types of program outcomes at both the organizational and participant levels.

During the formation, creation, and tweaking of the evaluation component of the project, it's important to keep a broad perspective in terms of consider-

Table 4.1. Examples of Outcome Measures

Example of outcome to be measured	How will it be measured?
Organizational: Improvements to infrastructure (e.g., accessibility)	Functional testing or checklists
Organizational: Collaborative and cooperative efforts to provide program opportunities	Record of active contacts; written agreements with other parties
Organizational: Activities implementation	Active log of scheduled and conducted activities
Organizational: Record of participation in activities	Attendance tallies; count of activities offered
Participant: Feelings about program's value	Baseline and comparison measure regarding attitude before and after program
Participant: Usefulness or value of information obtained from program	Follow-up measures on satisfaction
Participant: Intention to use library resources	Baseline and comparison measure of resource use before and after program
Participant: Residual impact on decisions or actions	Follow-up measures on how information has been used

Adapted from Burroughs & Wood, 2000.

ation of what types of data might be useful. If you are, for example, using survey questionnaires to evaluate a new approach to story time provision (whether it's different scheduling, inclusion of music and dance, etc.), although you may be evaluating a program targeted to a specific group (e.g., caregivers at story time), it may also make sense to include general demographic questions, since these data could be useful for future planning. Perhaps you'll discover that the majority of attendees are grandparents or are from a certain geographic area; having access to this type of information can in turn help guide outreach, marketing, and perhaps tailoring future programming efforts.

Another consideration is that if you're implementing a range of programs and want to know if participation in the programs has had a positive effect on attendees, it will likely be necessary to conduct some type of pre-test in order to determine the attendees' or participants' starting point with regard to the knowledge, behavior, or activity you're offering. In other words, baseline measures will be needed before the program begins so that comparisons can be made to assess changes after the program has been implemented. In some cases, the program itself might have built-in baseline measures that help prompt participants, as with the health promotion project at the Farmville Public Library, discussed in textbox below.

CHAPTER 4

READY-MADE BASELINE COLLECTION: USING CHART TO PROMOTE HEALTH

Some program opportunities have built-in baseline measures, such as in the case of a health promotion initiative conducted in concert with the Farmville Public Library. In 2014–2015, I worked with a rural public library director in eastern North Carolina to introduce pedometers and an individualized online health self-assessment program to local library users. After a successful pilot project with lending pedometers indicated patron interest in health initiatives, we provided access to an online health assessment tool, the Carolina Health Assessment Research Tool (CHART).

The CHART tool (https://chart.unc.edu) was designed by researchers at the University of North Carolina at Chapel Hill's Gillings School of Global Public Health to assess behavioral risk factors for cancer and other chronic health conditions, to improve participant/patient awareness and motivation to modify behavioral risks, and aid in launching interventions to reduce behavioral risks. CHART consists of a number of modules with questionnaires that result in a health summary with tips and suggestions for behavior change. The modules offered during this study included: physical activity, eating, alcohol use, tobacco use, and weight. The library director used strategic recruiting to include varying genders, ages, and ethnicities to identify ten participants for the study.

The selected participants were given access to the CHART tool; all ten completed the initial assessment on their own computers, though they were made aware that they could also use the library's computers if they preferred or needed to. The initial or baseline assessments were completed in April and May 2015. Anecdotal feedback on the initial baseline assessment included:

"I found the initial assessment website very easy to navigate. . . . It really served to acknowledge to me that I am headed in the right direction."
"It was easy to navigate. . . . It nudged me to open my eyes to my excuses as to why I had gained 10 lbs. . . . I had to really pay attention to what works for me. . . . I stopped breakfast and felt a lot better . . . and 'Wa-La' [sic] 5 lbs. thinner!"
"The use of the site was very easy. I liked that I could see my standing with others that are involved. For me, it validated information I already knew and validated changes I need to make. Yes I would say I felt encouraged to be healthier. . . . I'm glad to be apart [sic] of this study."
"I would like to thank you for letting me participate in the joint health and wellness project. Everything worked perfectly. It was a breeze going thru the website. I am even more encouraged to eat better and exercise more."

Approximately six months later, follow-up assessments were completed by nine of the same ten individuals (one participant was lost to follow-up) in November and December 2015.

Most categories remained similar between baseline and follow-up assessments. The question on weight for the follow-up assessment was an exception, however. For the six individuals out of nine who answered, four reported having lost weight (five, seven, sixteen, and twenty pounds); the other two reported having stayed within one pound of their weight between the two assessments. Reports of engaging in moderate physical activity increased across the sample as well.

For the nine individuals who completed the follow-up assessment, we also created and administered a short survey that included the following two questions specific to their experiences using the CHART tool:

1. Did finishing the first assessment make you pay more attention to your health (for example, did you pay more attention to your diet or physical activity levels)?
2. Did finishing the first assessment have any effect on your health behaviors (for example, diet, physical activity, interaction with healthcare provider)?

For both questions, five of nine participants answered *yes*. For question 1, comments offered for the affirmative responses included:

"Yes, became more thoughtful about activity and increasing it when I can. More thoughtful about healthy eating habits and changes I can make." (This individual reported having lost five pounds.)
"My weight, I weigh too much for my height."
"Somewhat, tried to do more fruits and vegs."
"Trying to pay more attention to diet; certainly have increased activity."
"Yes more careful on food purchases."

For affirmative responses to question 2, these additional comments were made:

"Increased my activity level."
"I am biking 20–30 minutes daily and walking has increased to at least an hour—average 15–17000 steps daily."
"Yes started paying attention to pedometer." (This individual also reported having lost twenty pounds).
"I eat more fruits and vegetables."
"Yes—diet."

CHAPTER 4

An additional question on the short survey asked: What types of health promotion activities would you like the library to provide, if any? The answers to this question focused on programs or activities related to nutrition (sample menus, portion size, cooking demos, eating for healthy living) and increasing activity levels (exercise groups, 5K run, workout videos, senior fitness opportunities). In this case, our short survey data provided patron input for a logical trajectory for future health initiatives and programs. Overall feedback included encouragement for more such opportunities; some claimed the health promotion activities not only improved their awareness but also supported healthy behavior change.

This example is provided not only to make the point that some programs have ready-made ways to conduct baseline assessments (and in fact, these baseline measures may be embedded as a component of the program), but also to make the point that this modest effort did seem to encourage participants on their path toward better health. Please note, however, that the CHART health assessment tool was provided through funding from a research grant for this project and is generally not readily available to the general public. Collaboration with local public health departments, universities with schools of public health, and engaged health practitioners may yield collaborative opportunities that involve access to health measures with similar tools.

For a full report of this study, including limitations and other health promotion activities at the Farmville Public Library, please see Flaherty, M. G., & Miller, D. (2016). "Rural Public Libraries as Community Change Agents: Opportunities for Health Promotion." *Journal of Education for Library and Information Science, 57*(2), 143–50.

Quantitative and Qualitative Approaches

Most practitioners working in the library field don't need to perform research in the formal sense: We need to answer basic questions about what we have done and how well it has worked. Yet even the most basic inquiries about our programs require a minimal framework of neutral logic in order to be valid. Knowing that last week you had a record number of attendees during a weekly program says little if you do not know if the attendance was driven by the popularity of that day's subject or by the fact that it was a peak summer day with heavy rains with lots of kids at home who needed an outing. The tools of basic research can help to figure things like this out.

There are extensive resources on research methods, and most ALA-accredited library and information science programs offer and/or require a class in research methods. A strong argument is currently being made that a single course may no longer be adequate to prepare library practitioners for their dual roles as information interlocutors who help evaluate research and librarians who perform and produce research in an increasingly data-driven world (Matusiak & Bright, 2020). More and more, accountability (fiscal as well as existential) is tied to numbers and outcomes, and while it's beyond the scope and intent of this volume to provide exhaustive coverage of differing research approaches, a brief review of the most common concepts and methods will help provide context for data collection, use, and reporting in terms of program assessment and evaluation.

Research falls into one of two main types, generally speaking: quantitative and qualitative; a mixed-methods approach combines the two. Quantitative measures are counts or numerical measures, which at their core are things that involve minimal subjective judgment. Attendance counts, program statistics, questionnaires, and surveys that use discrete numerical ratings would be classic examples of quantitative measures. Qualitative methods employ techniques such as interviews, focus groups, case studies, and observation in order to assess things that are, at their core, subjective. Are people happy or unhappy about something? Did an event induce hope? Do people prefer one kind of event over another? These are things that require assessing what people think or feel, and thus are usually not captured well by simple tallies or yes/no answers. There is often a great deal of overlap between these two kinds of data. Qualitative research generally uses language as its primary data resource in the way quantitative research utilizes numbers (Beck & Manuel, 2008). Table 4.2 outlines data collection methods with some of their concomitant advantages and disadvantages.

Of course, organizational resources (i.e., time, staff abilities, funds) will play a role in what data you collect and how you go about collecting, compiling, analyzing, and reporting them. Methodologically, however, the strongest approach is a mixed-methods approach, one that uses and reports both quantitative and qualitative measures. For example, a report that includes quotes from attendees along with attendance numbers will provide stronger evidence for interpreting, understanding, and communicating the value and impact of program efforts.

In addition to using tools such as attendance statistics and feedback from library users, consider using ancillary data to inform program and event planning and provision. For instance, keeping track of circulation and resource use by category of subject matter may signal community interest in a specific topic. So, if there's an uptick in gardening resources circulation, consider hosting a program, starting a seed library, or having a plant swap event to kick off the

Table 4.2. Data Collection Methods, Advantages, and Disadvantages

Method	Disadvantages	Advantages
Surveys and Questionnaires	Little flexibility once created; can be formulaic and miss key topics not understood by researchers beforehand	Can reach broad audience Can be answered anonymously Relatively low resource output Variety of tools readily available
Interviews or Focus groups	Time consuming; can be costly in terms of resources Difficult to reach large number; limits possible sample size Interviewee may want to be accommodating in answers	Allows for more flexibility and adaptation Can be better approach for nonnative speakers Allows for in-depth information collection
Observation	Observer's presence may affect outcomes Time consuming; can be costly in terms of resources (creating tools for documentation) Observers require training Difficult to reach large number; limits possible sample size Requires logistical planning	Can be viewed as a record of what actually occurred Allows for gaining unanticipated insights
Records or Documents Review	Time consuming; can be costly in terms of resources (e.g., staff time) Possible legal or ethical constraints with certain records (e.g., patron circulation records) Data may not be complete	Usually viewed as objective, and thus seen as reliable and credible Chronological record of events Unobtrusive approach Low staff impact if records are already being collected

spring season. In the same way, steady interlibrary loan requests on a specific topic may not only indicate a need to collect or provide more resources on a topic but may also help drive program opportunities.

Other Data Resources

All types of data sources can help inform program planning, provision, and evaluation. The list below describes some of those sources and how they might be used.

EVALUATION AND OUTCOME MEASURES

- Historical: Can be used for comparison purposes; what worked, what didn't?
- Geographic: Are there underserved areas in your catchment area? Are there features you can take advantage of, such as a nearby walking trail that could include a story walk?
- Transportation: Is the library readily accessible? Are there patrons who need assistance?
- Legal: Is the library building accessible? What is the capacity of your meeting room?
- Demographic: Are there societal segments you should target? Are there new community members to reach? Who in the community is networked to whom?
- Economic: What are the indicators in your community? What are the needs?
- Organizational: What resources are available?
- Educational and Social Organizations: Are there other groups in the community with whom you can work?
- Recreational and Cultural Organizations: Are there other groups in the community with whom you can collaborate?
- Other Information Services: Are you complementing services that are available?
- Community Planning Documents: These can help inform where things are headed; are there new initiatives under way?
- Anecdotal: Are patrons providing regular input? What is popular in the community? What kind of inquiries are most common at the reference or circulation desks?

Triangulation

In research, triangulation refers to comparing findings or indications from different data sources to see if they are suggesting the same conclusion. The more numerous the sources you can assess and the more disconnected or different in nature the data sources suggesting the same conclusion, the more likely the conclusion is correct. Combining data from different approaches creates a stronger picture and may provide a variety of ways to understand a phenomenon. This may mean combining methods like surveys and interviews with observation. In the example given above, where a specific program experienced a record number of attendees, if the staff looked through attendance records and found that two of the last three high-attendance days were also rainy days, that would

CHAPTER 4

suggest attendance was affected by the weather. But staff could also potentially contact ten of that event's participants who aren't regular attendees and have a chat with them about how it went, whether they enjoyed themselves, and if there was anything in particular that brought them in on that day. If nine out of ten say that they came in large part because it was rainy, then you have triangulated with both historical weather and attendance data as well as attendee interviews suggesting the same conclusion. While this is a trivial example, if you are going to buy snacks for forty people instead of twenty people and bring up extra seats from the basement, those ten calls might be a good investment before creating a new rainy day protocol. In this case, given that you have triangulated between very independent data sources, the chances that you are mistaken become very low. Triangulation generally leads to better confidence in the validity of each of the aligning measures and in your overall conclusions. Data can present themselves and be collected in a variety of forms, often informally, as described in the following examples in textboxes, where triangulation and information collection occurred somewhat naturally and serendipitously.

MAKING THE CASE FOR A NEW RESOURCE

In 2004, shortly after I started in my position as a public library director, we were considering introducing DVDs to our video offerings; at the time, VHS was the most common media in our rural community. Rather than dive right in with this "new" resource, we needed to collect data to help inform our decision. I started with discussing the notion at our bimonthly staff meeting (informal interviews). Some staff were worried about the video rental store that was about two blocks from the library and how this would impact their business. So I headed down to the store and asked the store owner (another informal interview—key informant) to share his thoughts about the possibility of the library making DVDs available to the community. He was delighted at the prospect and said that given the library would likely be collecting things that he didn't have enough circulation to warrant purchasing—"like BBC and *Mystery*"—we would not be infringing on his business in any way. He saw the move as encouraging the public to engage in media, not as competition for his business.

We decided to test the waters slowly, as we knew that in our area a majority of patrons did not yet have DVD players, and provided access to about ten DVDs in a variety of genres. We couldn't keep them on the shelves; they flew out of the library (circulation statistics). So we invested more of the collection budget in switching to this new resource item. We then tracked what percentage of circulation they accounted for and what percentage of the budget was allocated to the resource (more quantitative measures). We found that circulation increased 400 percent over three years for a resource that was around .01 percent of the budget.

Our final data point to justify expansion of the DVD collection came through observation of patron behavior, but in a somewhat unexpected manner. The library was in upstate New York, where winters are long and messy. When our janitor came in one day in March and asked if we could invest in new carpet mats for the path to where the DVD sleeves were housed, I realized our patrons were literally voting for the resource with their feet—they were bringing slush in on their boots that made a well-defined path on the carpet. This example demonstrates that research and data collection are regularly taking place in our day-to-day library operations and decision-making processes; we just don't always frame or characterize these routine activities as such.

From a program provision standpoint, the outcome some three to four years after the introduction of DVDs was institution of a monthly movie night with a speaker who introduced the showing (e.g., the local track coach introduced *Chariots of Fire*) and free popcorn (provided by the Friends of the Libraries and their popcorn machine). The attendance numbers and feedback from attendees demonstrated such enthusiasm for the program that it became a staple—with ongoing assessment and regular patron input, of course.

ROUTINE DATA COLLECTION

When the University of Chapel Hill Libraries were approached about hosting the annual campus-wide emergency response exercise in the library, one of the first considerations was: What would be the best time to schedule the exercise so that it caused the least disruption to library users and staff? The daily gate statistics that were regularly compiled by the circulation staff provided the necessary information. The statistics showed that the one day of intersession between the first and second summer semesters had the lowest gate count year after year. With this readily available data, it was clear which day and time would be the best for scheduling the emergency response exercise. Libraries of all types have to adapt scheduling and activities throughout the course of the year and have to adapt their services with changes in seasonal traffic patterns. Data such as gate count numbers and regular attendance counts can provide valuable guidance not just for scheduling and program assessment, but for all types of administrative decision-making.

CHAPTER 4

Data Mechanics

Once you've determined what it is that you want to know and what information you'll need from the data you collect, while taking into consideration what resources you can use for the process, it's time to settle on the logistics and particulars of how you will perform data collection. There are a number of readily available tools, some of which are briefly introduced here.

Questionnaires or surveys are often the default mechanism for collecting feedback from large numbers of participants. This is because they are efficient: They can be automated, they're versatile, and they cost relatively little. If you have a representative sample, this method can also be generalizable to a larger population. Possible hurdles with this approach are nonresponse, poor measurement, and an inadequate sample or sampling error.

When you choose a tool or create a questionnaire, remember to consider the respondents. In general, survey questions should avoid any confusing words or phrases and jargon, and should attempt to minimize risk of bias (by using specific trigger words), fence-sitting (by adding a neutral response), and floating (by giving the "I don't know" option). If you're using surveys and/or questionnaires, start by checking to see if your organization has a subscription to software that will support this (e.g., many organizations use Qualtrics, which also has options for free accounts). SurveyMonkey is another popular online tool that offers free access for launching surveys.

Decide ahead of time when you'll be administering any survey instruments and who will be responsible for administration; for example, is there a baseline knowledge or skill level assessment to prepare so that it can be completed before program participation? Build on existing instruments; there's no need to reinvent the wheel. Pre-test ahead of time and then refine your instrument based on feedback. Maintain the focus throughout, make the purpose clear, and limit response possibilities. Keep it simple, not only for respondents but for analysis. Along those lines, make it easy to submit and offer alternative submission mechanisms. Consider a small incentive, such as being entered in a raffle, if there's a need to increase response rates.

Many public library directors and staff report they are now using Project Outcome, developed by the ALA's Public Library Association. Project Outcome was developed as a free tool for public library staff to aid in assessment and measurement. The tool provides simple surveys and is an "easy-to-use process for measuring and analyzing outcomes" (ALA, 2020). It focuses on eight service areas, including: civic/community engagement, digital learning, economic development, education/lifelong learning, early childhood literacy, health, job skills, and summer reading. Project Outcome provides immediate and follow-up surveys, survey management tools, standardized outcome measures, data analytics, and access to training. A similar tool, Project Outcome for Academic Libraries, is managed by the Association of College & Research Libraries (ACRL). For more information on both of these programs, see https://www.projectoutcome.org.

GIVE 'EM WHAT THEY WANT

The sample goal from chapter 1—*Bring more young adults into the library*—and its accompanying objective—*As a result of participating in the Introduction to Juggling workshop, young adult attendees will be able to explain the basic components of circle juggling*—were actually borne out of my experience as a public library director. When I started at the library, there was a group of teens who liked to hang out on the library benches and use them as a de facto smoking salon. Many of the library staff members were intimidated by the group and gave them a wide berth. When patrons started complaining about the ambience, I realized we had to come up with some ideas for connecting with and serving this community group.

At the time, we had an enthusiastic and well-loved children's librarian. Her interest and focus were toddlers, preschoolers, and elementary-aged children. She had no interest in working with teens. It became apparent that if we were going to engage these young folks, it would be up to me. So, when the group converged on the benches, I regularly went out and struck up conversations with them. At first, some of the teens skedaddled (it was clear they did not want to be seen hanging out with the librarian), but those who remained were entertained that I was soliciting their input about how the library could serve them. There was a resounding prejudice about libraries as book repositories with a mission of promoting reading, with comments like, "We might as well be at school." When I asked about programs they might be interested in, they were bemused and a bit belligerent at first: "What could the library possibly offer that would be any fun?" I started cautiously, answering, "I don't know, maybe juggling workshops?" (I figured if their hands were busy, they'd be less likely to use them for lifting cigarettes to their mouths.) They were skeptical, and said something like, "Oh sure, and who's going to do that?" I said, "I will." After abiding their guffaws and smirks, I marched into the library and came out with three balls and proceeded to juggle on the front steps. That encounter led us to create and offer juggling workshops aimed at teens. We came up with our objective for the first workshop that included two indicators (number of attendees and their ability to explain basic components after the workshop), which helped us to determine whether we were reaching our goal.

CHAPTER 4

Figure 4.1 uses this example to demonstrate the different components and their relationship. Note that while the process is described as a cyclical one, outcomes (successful or not) will likely lead to revised and new goals and objectives, so this feedback loop is an ongoing enterprise. There may well be additional outcomes at the individual participant level (e.g., increased confidence; physical mastery of juggling) or the organizational level (e.g., creation of a library juggling team; participation on the library's teen advisory board).

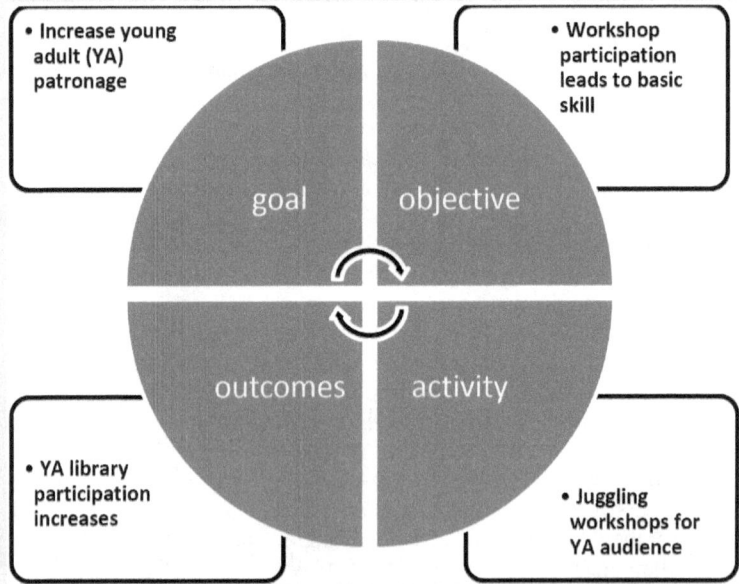

Figure 4.1. Intersection of goals, objectives, activities, and outcomes. *Courtesy of the author*

The workshops were a huge success and the group no longer congregated on the benches to smoke or hang out; instead we had created a regular group of about ten jugglers. The workshops laid the groundwork for bringing this community segment into the library, creating a teen advisory board, and the eventual hiring of an assistant director whose duties included serving as the teen and young adult services librarian. In the interest of full disclosure, I ran into one of our best jugglers a couple years ago—now twelve or thirteen years later—and he fondly remembered the program. He beamed, saying, "My friends can't believe that I can juggle!" I'm sorry to also report that our encounter was in a convenience store and he was purchasing cigarettes, reminding me that there are only so many outcomes we can influence.

EVALUATION AND OUTCOME MEASURES

Analysis

Automated survey tools, such as those available through resources such as Project Outcome and Qualtrics, have a built-in analysis component and supply summary reports as data are collected. Microsoft Excel can also be used for simple data analysis that entails descriptive statistics as well. There are numerous online tutorials and resources for help. Resources to help you get started are included below.

RECAP

In summary, evaluations are a necessary part of our institutions' activities, primarily because in this era of changing resources and patron expectations, evaluations are a key part of ensuring the quality of our services and programs. While no two libraries need exactly the same assessments, there are some common steps that we should follow. These include:

- Understanding and getting buy-in from key constituents regarding our goals
- Translating those goals into SMART objectives and indicators
- Assessing what data, resources, and possibilities are available to you
- Determining what methods will work best
- Assessing and triangulating those findings when possible
- Sharing those findings with your team and constituents as one of the many activities you will undertake to make your library serve your community

FURTHER RESOURCES

Demographic Data Resources

- Census American Fact Finder, https://factfinder.census.gov/
- Data USA, https://datausa.io/
- Local and state government websites
- Statistical Atlas, https://statisticalatlas.com/

CHAPTER 4

Research Approaches

Creswell, J. W., & Creswell, J. D. (2018). *Research Design: Qualitative, Quantitative, and Mixed Methods Approaches* (5th ed.). Los Angeles, CA: Sage.
Punch, K. F. (2013). *Introduction to Social Research: Quantitative and Qualitative Approaches* (3rd ed.). Los Angeles, CA: Sage.
Schutt, R. K. (2018). *Investigating the Social World: The Process and Practice of Research* (9th ed.). Los Angeles, CA: Sage.
Wildemuth, B. M. (2016). *Applications of Social Research Methods to Questions in Library and Information Science* (2nd ed.). Westport, CT: Libraries Unlimited.

For assistance using Excel for Statistical Analysis, the "For Dummies" series (e.g., *Excel Data Analysis for Dummies*, 2018) is a great starting point.

REFERENCES

American Library Association. (2020). "Performance Measurement, Introduction to Project Outcome." Public Library Association. Accessed August 23, 2020. http://www.ala.org/pla/initiatives/performancemeasurement
Barron, D. D., Williams, R. V., Bajjaly, S., Arns, J., & Wilson, S. (2005). *The Economic Impact of Public Libraries on South Carolina*. University of South Carolina. Accessed August 23, 2020. http://libsci.sc.edu/SCEIS/final%20report%2026%20january.pdf
Beck, S. E., & Manuel, K. (2008). *Practical Research Methods for Librarians and Information Professionals*. New York, NY: Neal Schuman.
Burroughs, C. M., & Wood, F. B. (2000). *Measuring the Difference: Guide to Planning and Evaluating Health Information Outreach*. Bethesda, MD: National Library of Medicine.
Diamond, D., Gillen, K. C., Litman, M., & Thornburgh, D. (2010). *The Economic Value of the Free Library in Philadelphia*. Fels Institute of Government. Accessed August 23, 2020. https://libwww.freelibrary.org/assets/pdf/about/fels-report.pdf.
Lance, K. C., & Kachel, D. E. (2018). "Why School Librarians Matter: What Years of Research Tell Us." *Phi Delta Kappan, 99*(7), 15–20.
Matusiak, K., & Bright, K. (2020). "Teaching Research Methods in Master's-Level LIS Programs: The United States Perspective." *Journal of Education for Library and Information Science, 61*(3), 357–82.

5

REPORTING THE RESULTS

Now that the planning, promoting, hosting, and evaluation of the program has occurred, it's time to tally and organize your results and share what you've found with your community. Reports are most often used for accountability to the public, funders, or other organizational authorities, and can be tailored for and targeted to different audiences and stakeholders. Thus, the term "reporting" will be used very broadly here. Annual reports often tabulate events, attendance numbers, and outcomes as a tool for articulating the community reach of the library. At the same time, ensuring a popular library event is covered in the local media with photos and favorable interviews from participants can be an extremely effective way to communicate the library's value while giving a positive boost to staff esprit de corps. Reporting can also be used as a powerful tool to promote the library, generate interest, celebrate successes, and share lessons learned.

This chapter covers ways to share results through communication with various stakeholders and addresses sharing results with the professional library community. It concludes with identifying outlets for reporting.

WHAT IS MEANT BY "REPORTING"?

As with program planning and evaluations, what is optimal for reporting on a program is determined by the goals of the program, the larger goals and responsibilities of the library, and the resources available. Thus, a program that

CHAPTER 5

involved a guest lecture on the amazing return of the bald eagle in the continental United States might be reported by attendance numbers, be it in an annual report or in a local newspaper article. Yet a program in the exact same room with the exact same attendees on how to participate in Cornell University's annual Great Backyard Bird Count would require some indication of intended attendee involvement or actual participation, or a comparison of local participation before and after the event.

In order to get a sense of what is typically happening presently with library program reporting in the online realm, two days in 2020 were randomly selected for review: one (January 28) before the widespread COVID-19 pandemic disruptions and one during (May 29). Google searches were conducted for items just from those two specific days. (Searches were performed on September 12, 2020.) Then, to assess the reporting that occurred later about the specific programs being announced or mentioned, two explorations were undertaken: a search of that library's website to see how it was reported and a separate, time-unconstrained Google search of that program at that library to see what was reported more widely on the internet. Thus, if the Spokane Public Library announced an upcoming seed program on January 28, an assessment was made months later of both what was reported by the library's website and what was reported on the internet using a Google search for "Spokane Public Library seed program." Reporting was broken into four broad categories: pictures and quotes or narratives, summary descriptions, numbers of attendees or activities (e.g., minutes spent reading by children), or no reporting. Some libraries may have had multiple reporting modes (e.g., pictures and a summary).

Excluding ads, fifty-one hits were found for "library program" on those two days, sixteen of which appeared to be about specific events or programs. Of those sixteen, the two corresponding search processes revealed no reporting for ten. Four reported with photographs or narratives. Three reports were general summaries, and only two included attendee numbers. It may not be unexpected or inappropriate that two-thirds of libraries appear to not be reporting. For example, in describing its summer reading program, the library system in Bolivar County, Mississippi, rightly cited that summer reading programs have been shown to keep children's reading abilities from atrophying during the break from school attendance. Given the benefit of a program has been widely proven and acknowledged, it may not be necessary to report extensive outcome details. Moreover, with summer reading and other programs, while participant numbers are not available on the library's website, it is highly likely they are recorded, used, and shared elsewhere.

Lack of reporting with library programs is in some cases similar to the absence of reports regarding the use of a local bridge; the lack of reporting occurs because the value of the service is universally accepted and taken for granted. For a program at the University of Minnesota that has the purpose of helping to advance the careers of young librarians, only a picture of all the gleeful attendees appears on the website, with no descriptive narrative or attendance numbers. In terms of the website reporting objectives, this picture was likely the perfect way to share the results in that it implied robust attendance numbers to any fiscally focused administrators, and it exuded satisfaction and joy from the attendees—the perfect recruitment message for potential attendees to next year's program. Perhaps not by chance, the program announcement in the results that seemed to have the most press coverage raised a related article in the Google search revealing that the library won an outreach grant for more than a million dollars seven months later. Thus, reporting may have indirect benefits as well.

In summary, once a program has occurred, good reporting means communicating the objectives of the program and the library's mission. The degree to which this can be described as an art rather than a science will be elucidated by the topics and examples that follow.

Responsibility

In many cases, staff responsibility for report compilation will be obvious. For instance, usually annual reports to funders and/or state agencies are ultimately the director's responsibility, even if duties related to the report are delegated across departments or divisions. With programs, report writing may be up to the services coordinator or the staff member who conceived of and hosted the program, or it may be in the domain of the outreach staff or communications department.

If reporting duties are not readily described and/or ascribed in existing job descriptions, make sure before the program is launched that there's a clear delineation of duties and that this is communicated transparently ahead of time with staff. This way, when it comes to writing the report, there will be explicit ownership, and the responsibility for recording and sharing results won't be overlooked. In addition, allow for training and resources for staff who are tasked with creating reports, such as opportunities to engage in workshops on topics like maximizing use of digital photography and website usability and design.

CHAPTER 5

Basic Elements

Almost a hundred years ago, the library literature included discussions of the need for "modern" annual reports about library services for the general public. Munn (1923) was one of the first librarians to recognize the utility of library reporting for publicity purposes. He suggested creating two reports, one that would serve as the "document of record" and a second pamphlet-type publication that would highlight the library's work over the course of the year. This would include statistics "made interesting through graphic presentation" (Riffey, 1952, p. 4). In *Library Journal* in 1938, Juanima Wells, librarian of the Bexar County Free Library in San Antonio, Texas, also advocated for interesting, lively, graphic reports, not "bloodless statistics" (p. 13), to demonstrate the value of the library as a tax-supported institution. The need for a combination of reporting quantitative and qualitative data was already recognized by the midpoint of the twentieth century. It was widely agreed that there was a need to produce attractive, readable, and engaging library reports that would foster positive public relations with regard to library support.

Although we use "reporting" in this chapter in a broader, less formal sense, there are key features that are timeless and are included in most types of written reports. Written reports:

- are directed to a specific audience,
- are fact based,
- have a clear structure,
- use graphics (e.g., tables, charts, pictures) to make points,
- include a summary highlighting the main points,
- and have supporting data as appendices (e.g., survey examples).

INFORMING STAKEHOLDERS

Stakeholders are the individuals and entities who have some type of interest in the organization generally and, in this case, programs specifically. They can affect and are affected by the library's choices. Stakeholders with a possible interest in program reports generally fall into three categories: library users, the greater community, and funders or sponsors (who may overlap with oversight).

Library Users

The library's users, whether regular program participants or not, are usually a primary focus or audience for sharing reports of library programs and activities; collaborators, whether past, current, or future, are also included in the list of regular recipients of library news. Consider tailoring reports to share with a specific audience if you don't already do so. For example, if you've hosted a program for emergency responders on the use of apps that are available from the National Library of Medicine for disaster planning and response (https://disasterinfo.nlm.nih.gov/apps), beyond the regular channels of sharing results, a brief summary of the program outcomes could be shared with the local fire chief or safety officer.

Greater Community

Depending on library type, the oversight committee may be an appointed or elected board, a group of supervisors, a faculty committee, the dean or provost, the mayor, or library system board. As mentioned earlier, there may also be mandated reporting requirements depending on the library setting and situation. Beyond the required data sharing, keeping the library's activities on the community's radar screen is an effective way to generate interest and establish the library as a vital, necessary resource.

Potential users are another important consideration when planning for and reviewing outlets for reporting. Is there a segment of your community that you are missing? What are the best channels for reaching them? Perhaps it's placing posters in local stores, beauty salons, or barbershops, or hosting pop-up events in local preschools or clinics.

Funders

If a program is supported by external funding—through grant and/or gift support from institutions such as state or federal government agencies or foundations, for example—there will be specified reporting requirements. Reports may be required quarterly, annually, or at other intervals. In this case, the emphasis of reporting is usually fiscal accountability, and the library staff has to demonstrate they were good stewards of any funds received, with precise reporting of how funds were spent. Good record keeping along the way is essential and helps immensely with this type of reporting.

CHAPTER 5

The example below isn't specifically related to reporting on a library event. It is included here because it's a great example of effective communication with the community around a difficult issue and it involves the use of the library's meeting room; thus, it qualifies as a form of reporting and sharing information with the library's stakeholders.

TROUBLE IN TORONTO

In the fall semester of 2017, I was teaching the required core graduate library science course Resource Selection and Evaluation when the Toronto Public Library was in the news with regard to community room bookings. The director, Vickery Bowles, was an acquaintance from our previous time together on an International Federation of Library Associations and Institutions (IFLA) committee, so I e-mailed her to ask if she could provide some information on the situation to share with the class. Our subsequent e-mail exchange on September 13, 2017, is included here.

> Hi Vickery,
> I hope this note finds you well.
> We were discussing different issues and policies in public libraries in the collection development class yesterday, and one of our students (a Canadian) mentioned the meeting room dilemma for the memorial service you recently faced.
> They asked me to inquire a bit about the process that took place in your decision-making process to allow the event to take place, and just what that conversation entailed, and security measures, etc.
> No worries if you're too busy to get into this, I just mentioned that I did know you, and would see if we could get more details on how decisions like this are addressed. Thanks so much!
>
> All best,
> Mary Grace

Here is Vickery's reply:

> Hi Mary Grace,
> It is so good to hear from you. I am glad to give you background on our room booking issue. Certainly it is relevant to collections and intellectual freedom values. If this had been a white supremacist rally, we would not have allowed it . . . but it was a memorial service. Here is some information:
>
> *Background*
> On July 12, 2017, there was a community space rental at the Richview branch which garnered a great deal of attention from the public, the media,

88

and local politicians. This third-party room booking was made approximately three weeks prior to the event. Toronto Public Library (TPL) learned on July 11, 2017, that the booking was for a memorial for Barbara Kulaszka, a lawyer known for her work on free speech cases involving far right causes including white supremacists.

People became aware of the event because it was posted on at least two websites.

Regarding the July 12 booking for the memorial event, TPL received legal advice from City of Toronto Legal Services. The legal advice confirmed TPL does not have the grounds to deny the booking. To deny access to library spaces on the basis of the views or opinions that individuals or groups have expressed in the past contravenes the *Canadian Charter of Rights and Freedoms*. From the Library's perspective, values enshrined in the Charter and in particular, the principles of intellectual freedom, are core to the Library's mission and values.

Based on the information available and considering TPL's policies and the legal opinion received, TPL decided to maintain the room booking as the nature of the event itself (a memorial) was not in contravention of TPL's Rules of Conduct, the Community and Event Space Rental policy, or the law. TPL also determined that it would not be reasonable to assume that this event would contravene law or TPL policy based on what someone may say during the event or based on what has been stated in the past by attendees.

TPL received a lot of feedback from the public, which was predominantly negative.

TPL issued this statement on its webpage defending the decision to allow the room booking to proceed:

I'd like to address the issue about last evening's private room booking event at Richview Library, which has received tremendous attention. It has been a difficult situation, but one that we've been guided through by our library values.

First, a little bit of background. This event was booked as a third-party rental booking approximately three weeks ago. We learned on Tuesday that it was to be a memorial for Barbara Kulaszka, a lawyer known for her work with far right causes and free speech cases. As word got out, we received hundreds of emails, phone calls and social media messages calling for us to cancel the booking. The general theme was that people felt that by upholding the booking we were endorsing the views of the individuals that were organizing the meeting, individuals who have extreme white nationalist views.

We heard and understood these concerns, and assessed the situation from a legal, library and public perspective. As you know, we do not tolerate hate speech. However, we cannot deny bookings that are in accordance with the law and the library's policy and rules of conduct.

To deny access on the basis of the views or opinions that individuals or groups hold contravenes the Canadian Charter of Rights and Freedoms and the principles of intellectual freedom, both cornerstones

CHAPTER 5

> of the library's mission and values. Sometimes in defending freedom of speech, it's very uncomfortable to be put in a situation where we are defending the rights of those whose viewpoints many consider to be offensive. However, it is at those times that we must be vigilant in protecting the rights of all.
> We were prepared to take immediate action should the group have acted in a manner that was not consistent with the law or our rules of conduct. We had a staff member attend the event to monitor it to ensure no laws or rules of conduct were contravened. We had a protocol in place to shut down the meeting if there was any hate speech. About 20 people attended the memorial service and staff talked to the organizers in advance of the meeting to reiterate our expectations. The group did not violate any laws or rules, and had a memorial service as originally indicated.
> The Mayor has asked us in a statement to review our room booking policy, which we will do at an upcoming Toronto Public Library Board meeting this fall. These are open meetings and everyone is welcome to attend.
> I strongly believe the right decision was made to allow the memorial to proceed. In making this decision we had to find a way for the Library to ensure the group's legal rights to gather and to free speech while protecting against discrimination, harassment and hate speech.
> As difficult as this situation has been, it is also a strong reminder of public library values.

Hope this is helpful.
All the best,
Vickery
Vickery Bowles, City Librarian
Toronto Public Library

Professional Sharing

There are well-known, inherent challenges in our broad and varied library and information science field in terms of sharing information across academic and practitioner silos. Due to cost or other considerations, those who research library services and issues are generally reporting in venues that might not be used by the folks who are running libraries and information centers. Likewise, running a library leaves little time for extensive reporting beyond required mechanisms. However, it is vital to be actively involved in the professional organizations related to your library type and interests and to support professional membership and involvement among your staff.

The access to resources and opportunities for sharing ideas (e.g., through publications, informational forums for members, and conference venues) that comes from membership in organizations such as the Medical Library Association, the Special Library Association, divisions of the American Library Association (such as the Public Library Association and the Young Adult Library Services Association), state and regional library associations, the Association for Rural and Small Libraries, the Urban Library Council, and so on—a comprehensive list of various professional organizations is too numerous to include here—is well worth the price of membership. Other opportunities for sharing ideas and program results are available through forums such as Let's Move in Libraries (https://letsmovelibraries.org/), a resource for promoting healthy living through public libraries.

Just as it is important to share examples of successful programs and initiatives with our colleagues and peers, it is vital to share the lessons we learn when things don't go as expected as well. The example in the next textbox describes an outreach program initiative that encountered a number of challenges along the way—and how they were ultimately overcome.

LESSONS LEARNED: ADAPTING AN OUTREACH PROGRAM

As director of the Sidney Memorial Public Library in rural Upstate New York in the mid-2000s, I was successful in securing a Health Information System grant from the National Library of Medicine (NLM). The funding provided support for outreach to local hospital staff and rural health care providers to train them on the use of NLM resources for locating and using authoritative health information. As reported elsewhere (Flaherty & Roberts, 2009; Flaherty, 2017), there were a number of unexpected hurdles over the course of the three-year project. At the conclusion of the project, we summarized our adaptations, wrote about the completed project, and submitted our manuscript to a peer-reviewed journal. Upon review, two of the reviewers commented on the importance of recording and reporting "lessons learned"; one stated that all too often we codify our successes, when there can be just as much (if not more) to learn from the hurdles we overcome when programs don't proceed as planned.

A brief summary of how the project transpired is included here to demonstrate how the program evolved and what reporting mechanisms were used to share our outcomes.

The project was initiated after I met with local healthcare providers and four regional hospital administrators. As a result of those meetings, we determined there was an interest in and a need for assistance with accessing, evaluating, and procuring health information among healthcare staff at all

CHAPTER 5

levels. With this information in hand, I proceeded with the application to NLM for funding to support a regional health outreach project.
The objectives for the project included:

1. To increase access to quality health-related information for end users, including consumers, physicians, and healthcare staff
2. To provide training to local hospital staff, healthcare providers, and end users in effective utilization of the databases and resources provided by NLM
3. To provide document delivery as required to rural healthcare providers
4. To evaluate the effectiveness of a health information outreach training program for rural library users, healthcare consumers, and healthcare providers

Measurement of the objectives included attendance numbers, baseline surveys, and post-training session surveys. In some cases, follow-up phone surveys were administered one year post-training. We used tracking software on our project-provided computer workstations that allowed anonymous evaluation of searching behaviors at the project sites. We also kept track of requested and fulfilled document requests, and reference requests for health information.

Besides our required regular reporting mechanisms (library newsletter and website, local media, monthly library board meetings, NLM biannual and final reports, financial reports to external auditor and to New York State), we also used the following reporting venues to share news of the project and our results:

- New York Library Association (NYLA) Annual Conference, 2005
  - Engaged in panel discussion where we described the project and presented on locating authoritative health information via online sources
- International Federation of Library Associations and Institutions (IFLA) Annual Conference, 2009
  - Panel participant, presented on the completed project and lessons learned: Flaherty, M. G. "Outreach for Rural Public Library Staff: An Effective Means for Consumer Health Information Dissemination." *Proceedings of the IFLA 75th General Conference and Council.* August 21–26, 2009, Milan, Italy.
- Submission to peer-reviewed journal in library information science field
  - Flaherty, M. G., & Roberts, L. (2009). "Rural Outreach Training Efforts to Clinicians and Public Library Staff: NLM Resource Promotion." *Journal of Consumer Health on the Internet, 13*(1), 14–30.

- Health Science Information Class (INLS:705, University of North Carolina at Chapel Hill, School of Information and Library Science)
  ○ Regularly use example in class lectures and as a case study exercise
- Summary in professional handbook, 2017
  ○ Flaherty, M. G. (2017). *The Library Staff Development Handbook: How to Maximize Your Library's Most Important Resource*. Medical Library Association Handbook Series. Lanham, MD: Rowman & Littlefield, pp.118–19.

This example is used to make the point that some, if not most, of our lessons are hard earned. We have the professional responsibility to share them through a variety of venues with our colleagues and future practitioners in order to help them identify potential pitfalls and to plan accordingly.

REPORTING OUTLETS

Every library and organization likely has standard communication streams tailored to its user community already in place. Depending on the community, these may be the library's webpage, organizational reports, local news outlets, and even locally placed bulletin boards. Social media resources (e.g., Facebook, Twitter, Instagram) have become increasingly important as libraries have had to adapt services during the COVID-19 pandemic, and are an easy, low-cost way to connect with and inform users of library news and services. Keep in mind, however, that as of 2019, approximately 30 percent of people in the United States aren't social media users (Perrin & Anderson, 2019), so you may be missing a segment of your community if you rely solely upon social media outlets for reporting.

Thinking Outside the Box

There are countless ways to report results beyond the commonly used tools and standard communication streams and outlets. In New York State, public libraries are required to compile annual data in a number of categories (i.e., budget, circulation, program attendance, etc.) and to submit the compilation to the state and report the results to their communities. After the Guernsey Memorial Library in Norwich, New York, compiled the annual data for its required state reports, the library shared the results with the community by engaging award-winning children's author Suzanne Bloom to create a visual representation of

CHAPTER 5

the results. The resultant graphic could then be used for posters in the library and throughout the town, for paper placemats in local restaurants and diners, and for coloring pages for storytime activities and in local preschools. What might otherwise have been a somewhat dull list of statistics and data became a lively depiction of vibrant service provision that was shared widely. Figure 5.1 is an example of one of the graphics.

Figure 5.1. Reporting with graphics. *Courtesy of Suzanne Bloom*

RECAP

Once programs are completed, it's easy to set the experience aside and move on to the next task or project. Before doing so, though, it's important to reflect upon what went right, what went wrong, and what changes can be made. Codifying these reflections and sharing them through reporting is necessary for progress; in this way, we can help to ensure a meaningful path forward with successful programs in the future.

REFERENCES

Munn, R. (1923). "Library Reports." *Library Journal*, 48, 413–14.
Perrin, A., & Anderson, M. (2019, April 10). "Share of Adults Using Social Media, Including Facebook, Is Mostly Unchanged since 2018." Pew Research Center,

FactTank: News in the Numbers. Accessed September 1, 2020. https://www.pewre search.org/fact-tank/2019/04/10/share-of-u-s-adults-using-social-media-including -facebook-is-mostly-unchanged-since-2018/

Riffey, M. S. (1952). "Annual Reports for Public Libraries." *University of Illinois Library School Occasional Papers, 28,* 1–23.

Wells, J. (1938). "Modernistic Library Records." *Library Journal, 63,* 11–13.

6

USING DATA TO INFORM SERVICE PROVISION

The importance of collecting program data and ways to do so were addressed in chapter 4, and different ways of sharing and reporting program data were discussed in chapter 5. Once efforts have been made to collect and report program data, the next step is to examine and use what you've discovered to tweak and improve your services. This chapter describes what is meant by "success" when it comes to programs, using data to ferret out opportunities for improvement and implementing those opportunities.

WHAT CONSTITUTES SUCCESS?

Success is generally defined as accomplishing some purpose or a specific aim. For librarians, success usually falls into broad categories: success in the patrons' view and success in the view of supporters (i.e., donors or program instigators). When the Gates Foundation donated thousands of computers to public libraries across the country two decades ago, the feedback they wanted was about numbers of library staff trained and computers available to the public. The foundation's aim was to increase public computer access (specifically, Microsoft-based computer access) geographically and to the less digitally empowered segments of society. This required data about geography combined with economic and internet access information. If one of those Gates-computer-recipient libraries held computer literacy training for the public, its aims were likely focused on the happiness, empowerment, and skill acquisition of the attendees. When thinking about placing computers in libraries, the Gates Foundation would likely use

CHAPTER 6

data for making big-picture training and distribution policies, while the libraries would use data collected to improve their training techniques and tweak their public outreach strategy.

Thus, when we apply this definition of achieving a purpose or aim to assessing library programs, there are potentially a number of measures related to predetermined goals and objectives that will help gauge the level of success on multiple levels. These measures can help to determine where adjustments can be made for future efforts.

Beyond achieving a specific purpose or aim, success involves other components as well (Yost, 2020). These include properly setting concrete goals, always doing your best, overcoming fear, not giving up, celebrating small victories, and understanding that you can't control everything.

Properly setting concrete goals is crucial, as knowing what you want to accomplish ahead of time helps guide your appraisal of success. A series of smaller, attainable goals and objectives lead to achieving larger goals, and well-constructed goals and objectives provide a framework with specific, tangible ways to measure outcomes. Though it may seem trite, *always doing your best*, no matter the program or initiative, is also imperative. Even if a program or event hasn't gone the way you expected, if you've truly put forth your best effort, you are personally successful and the library or organization will have been well represented. Keep in mind, too, that there may be ripple effects that aren't readily identifiable in the short-term and that won't ever be known to you (e.g., the citizen science program that inspired a high schooler to study ornithology in college).

Another important component for success, both on an organizational and on a personal level, is *overcoming fear*. Don't be afraid to try something new or with a different approach, as being open to new approaches and possibilities creates unforeseen opportunities. The old adage "Nothing ventured, nothing gained" applies here, as success does come to those who are willing to take calculated risks. If you're in a supervisory position, modeling reasonable, informed risk taking is essential. Keep in mind, too, what those risks might be—for hosting a program, the most obvious one is that there will be no interest or that no one will attend. While this may certainly be frustrating and disappointing after investing resources such as time, energy, and personal/organizational commitment, it won't derail library operations and will provide feedback from the community for future planning.

Along the same lines, *not giving up* is integral to success. Even if your first attempts at initiating a new series of programs don't work, they are laying the groundwork for future endeavors. Use what you've learned and try again. For instance, if you've tried to create a new schedule for story time to attract new families and have had low attendance, consider hosting a pajama story time in the early evening so that working parents can join.

It's important to *celebrate small victories* along the way. This approach helps optimism to flourish, has a positive impact on morale, and keeps momentum flowing in an upbeat manner. Remember, too, that *understanding you can't control everything* is also an important component of success. There will always be external factors (e.g., pandemics, weather events, etc.) that have an impact on programs that are well beyond your influence or control. When unforeseen hiccups occur, try to roll with it, keep calm, marshal your resources, support your colleagues, and do your best.

In the next Programming in Action example, Farmville Public Library director David Miller shares one of the library's successful health programming ventures, Walk With Ease, undertaken in collaboration with the local Parks and Recreation Department.

PROGRAMMING IN ACTION: THE OPPORTUNITY TO SERVE

Farmville Public Library, located in rural eastern North Carolina, serves as a trusted information center for the community of Farmville, made up of forty-six hundred citizens, as well as neighboring towns. Because of its rural geography, access to healthcare is limited and wellness opportunities for adults have traditionally been available only in a mid-sized city located twenty minutes away along the interstate, which is inconvenient for some. As an institution that strives to create a variety of learning opportunities for its community, the library views its rural geography and lack of readily available health opportunities as an opportunity to use its status as a learning center to serve as a community change agent for the health and well-being of all residents of its community.

Since 2014, the library has forged several partnerships with health and wellness organizations to implement many programs and collections to educate its community and create healthy lifestyles. One such learning opportunity that has proven itself to be successful and beneficial to its program participants and their families is the Walk With Ease program (https://www.arthritis.org/health-wellness/healthy-living/physical-activity/walking/walk-with-ease). Developed by the Arthritis Foundation and geared toward older adults who struggle with arthritis, the Walk With Ease program provides informational tools meant to reduce pain and discomfort, increase balance and strength, create a supportive opportunity to socialize with others who struggle with arthritis, and improve overall health and well-being.

CHAPTER 6

Curriculum

To address Farmville residents who struggle with arthritis, staff from the library and Farmville Parks and Recreation became certified leaders for this program through remote training and testing. The curriculum is a structured six-week program that is held three days per week; each session is broken into the following sections: group sharing, an educational lecturette led by library staff, stretching, walking, cooldown, and reflection. In addition, the library provides trustworthy information by utilizing its mobile pop-up library at each program to offer current and authoritative books for checkout pertaining to arthritis, cooking, fitness, and other health topics. Participants meet outdoors at a town government–maintained and ADA-accessible walking path that is equipped with a shelter and picnic tables in order to reap the health benefits of spending time outdoors, though the program has been led in Farmville's local community center during inclement weather.

Pre-Survey Data

As with all of its programs, the library collects before and after data through surveys and direct communication to gauge its effectiveness and lasting benefits for its participants. Thirteen individuals who participated in the first cohort, which ran through September and October 2019, completed a pre-survey at the start of the first session. The survey showed that the average age of individuals was seventy; eleven individuals stated they walked at least three times per week, twelve individuals indicated that they had chronic conditions, and all participants listed an average of 6 on a scale of 1 to 10 when rating their confidence in their ability to manage pain. All thirteen participants attended the vast majority of all of the sessions, and some attended all of the sessions.

Post-Survey Data

Participants completed a post-program survey at the end of the last session. Responses showed that participants increased their knowledge to manage pain to 8.5 on a scale of 1 to 10, all participants reported that their knowledge about managing arthritis increased, and all stated that they would recommend the program to a friend. Participants also checked out a total of forty-three health and wellness books from the mobile pop-up library that was set up at each session, and two individuals became new library users. In addition, participants were contacted directly one year later to see if the program has continued to be useful to them and their ability to manage their arthritis. One participant stated that "Walk With Ease continues to remind me how important it is to walk on a regular basis. My own pace is fine; just keep moving and stretching," and another stated that "I learned that continuing a walking program is beneficial for continued good health. Also, the program gave useful tips, like stretching before and after walking."

Empirical evidence gathered by library and Parks and Recreation staff also showed that the Walk With Ease program served as a valuable opportunity for individuals managing arthritis to meet others who are dealing with the same health issues. In some cases, new friendships were formed that have generated walking partnerships that continue one year later. In addition, participants and their family members expressed gratitude to both the library and Parks and Recreation for partnering to offer this program.

Farmville Public Library and Farmville Parks and Recreation are currently (as of this writing, in fall 2020) instructing the program's third cohort of ten new individuals and three individuals who participated in the program previously but saw the benefits and wanted to continue their journey in managing arthritis.

David Miller, MLIS
Director
Farmville Public Library
Farmville, North Carolina

FINDING OPPORTUNITIES FOR IMPROVEMENT

If you have planned ahead and already built an evaluation component into your program, there should be readily available data to assess program-goers' responses to your offerings. With in-person venues, there's a captive audience, so soliciting additional feedback can be as simple as distributing index cards to individuals with checkboxes or thumbs-up/thumbs-down significations after an event or providing a link to an online survey participants can complete within days of attending. However crude or simplistic such feedback may seem, it gives a logical, neutral, respectful way to compare the value to attendees between programs. If there are multiple elements within the evaluation (e.g., one speaker is assessed separately from another, a discussion session versus a formal presentation section), however rudimentary the assessment tool may be, one will likely have a valid assessment of how comparatively valuable the attendees found the various elements of the program. Including a question about where attendees learned about the program could help guide future marketing efforts.

CHAPTER 6

Staff who were involved in the program and in attendance can also provide their candid feedback: What was the overall "vibe" of the group? Did folks seem bored or engaged, happy, anxious, etc.? What did the body language of attendees imply? Encouraging staff to record their answer to these open-ended questions immediately post-program provides data (although somewhat subjective, it could still add to the overall appraisal to help guide future initiatives) and allows staff to describe their perception of how things went while the event is still fresh in their minds. If a number of staff who attended provide this feedback, responses can jump-start a discussion of this type of assessment and ways to tweak data collection.

Other observations staff could track are the general demographic makeup of attendees: new age groups, new faces, and so on. If you were expecting a high number of young adults to attend, but the room is filled with seniors, perhaps you didn't reach a segment of the community with your marketing efforts or offered it at a problematic time of day for the target group. Again, these data may be highly subjective, but they can provide an additional data point to consider within the context of the other data that have been collected and will help to ensure that staff are engaged in the process.

Figure 6.1 is a simple representation of a few different evaluative components to keep in mind when assessing program success. In this hypothetical example, after many community members expressed interest, an adult yoga program was offered. Survey evaluations were distributed for participants' reactions, which were then compiled and included in program reports. Attendance counts were recorded by staff who participated, and participant levels of enthusiasm were estimated and recorded as well. The third component, experience, is based on participants' estimation of skill acquisition after participation and will be captured with follow-up surveys.

Depending on the security of the library setting, you might consider installing an old-school suggestion box at the self-checkout station or at the service desk to solicit ideas from patrons. Perhaps you could hold a contest for the most innovative (or fun, or original, etc.) suggestion. If you do use such a tool, ensure that someone has responsibility for regularly checking the input that's been received and reporting back or acting upon it.

Program evaluation isn't an exact science, and some measures of success can be difficult to capture. There may be hidden benefits to a program that aren't highly visible or may not be codified or recorded. For instance, a patron who attended the library's nutrition workshop may have learned and applied new approaches for healthier eating and lowered their cholesterol, but this result might never be made apparent to the program hosts or organizers. Along those lines,

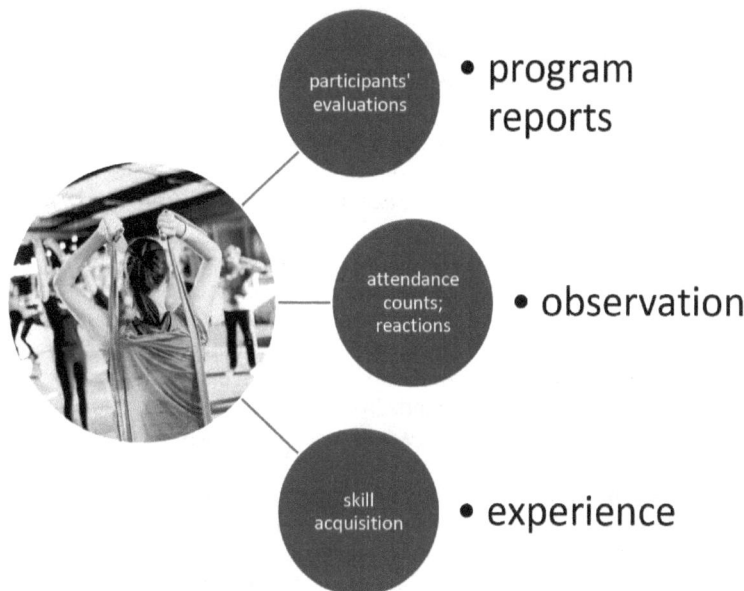

Figure 6.1. Evaluative components. *Unsplash by Geert Pieters*

assessments in the developing world suggest that the main benefit of teaching girls to read is that their children will be more likely to survive decades later. In another example, the initial Westinghouse study (sponsored by the Office of Economic Security) that set out to assess Head Start found no benefit after five years (Westinghouse Learning Corporation, 1969), but eventually it was revealed that the benefits of this childhood feeding program were profound when participants were in high school twelve to fifteen years later (Datta, 1982).

Thus, given the abstract and cerebral nature of what we do as librarians, on some level we need to accept that perhaps we cannot assess the most profound outcomes that we might empower (e.g., personal fulfillment, curiosity, social engagement). This makes it all the more important to collect data on simple and tangible measures of our programs like participant enjoyment and skill development. In this way, we can be constantly revising our efforts to be better, in the hopes of maximizing the chance that those long-term positive impacts we cannot measure will arise.

The next Programming in Action feature describes a collaborative community initiative in Johnson County, Indiana, that was in direct response to the region's health challenges, one that can easily be adapted for ready deployment in most communities.

CHAPTER 6

PROGRAMMING IN ACTION:
WALKTOBER IN JOHNSON COUNTY, INDIANA

In October 2020, the Johnson County Public Library, in collaboration with a coalition of local health leaders engaged in community health initiatives and support (Partnership for a Healthier Johnson County, https://www.healthierjc.org/about-us/), conducted the monthlong, all-ages walking campaign WALKtober (https://www.pageafterpage.org/walktober). The goal of the program, which was borne out of a response to alarming statistics with regard to residents' activity levels, was to "get more people out of the house, exercising while staying safe during the coronavirus pandemic." Almost a quarter of adults (ages twenty and over) in the county reported no leisure time physical activity; guidelines recommend at least 150 minutes per week of physical activity for adults, and youth (ages six to seventeen) should have at least an hour of physical activity daily (Trares, 2020).

The collaboration with the library was instrumental in making the campaign possible. A local branch manager is a member of the Partnership for a Healthier Johnson County's wellness team, and she shared the idea, which was already an established program at her library. The library also has a wellness team that had been regularly hosting an annual walk in October and found it to be one of the library's most popular offerings. The program was expanded and modified to reach a larger audience. The library uses the same app (Beanstack) for sign-up and recording activities as it does for summer reading and other events.

Activities during the monthlong promotion included the chance to earn prizes by signing up and logging activities. The campaign included challenges, such as visiting a local trail or completing a scavenger hunt. There was even a seasonally themed haunted trail—it is WALKtober, after all! After engaging in three weekly activities, participants earned a virtual badge and were entered in weekly drawings for prizes supplied by donations from local organizations and businesses. There were also weekly walking challenges and suggestions to check off (e.g., downtown trail systems, the local lake, story walks, parks, local murals) to keep interest in the program high. The library provided ideas and ensured that every town and area in the county was included. With the weekly challenges and opportunities for making suggestions, there was a built-in feedback loop to integrate program data seamlessly. It's easy to imagine all sorts of data collection and opportunities to involve participants:

- Total numbers of miles walked
  - By age groups, grade levels, organizations, etc.
  - By length, e.g., how far would the combined community miles extend (if we head west, can we reach Illinois; can we make it to the East Coast?); this could be promoted with an interactive map

- Voting for "best" trail, based on factors proposed by walkers
  - Most spectacular fall foliage
  - Most (or least) physically challenging
  - Most fun
  - Most colorful mural
  - Best story
  - And so on
- Other physical measures (as folks are willing to share; these can be aggregated to ensure anonymity)
- Total calories burned per participant (this could be summed up for the whole community on a regular basis and presented in promotional materials, with something like: Johnson County burned up 200,000 calories last week; that's equivalent to over 50 pounds!)
- Weight loss, sleep improvement, etc.
- Suggestions for additional activities
  - This could spur other community health initiatives that haven't yet been considered

The program was well promoted in local news outlets, and the *Daily Journal* newspaper provided a wonderful description, ending with a succinct "at a glance" summary to guide residents, listing what, who, and how it works. A few days before the program's October 1 kickoff, organizers reported that more than two hundred people had already signed up. This is the type of activity that can involve the entire community, from health organizations to local businesses to school groups; everyone wins.

Programs like WALKtober are happening at libraries throughout the country, and organizations such as the nonprofit America Walks (https://americawalks.org/) offer small grants (e.g., Community Change Grants) to jump-start projects that help create "healthy, active, and engaged places to live, work, and play." The Safe Routes Partnership (https://www.saferoutespartnership.org/) is another nonprofit that promotes safe walking in order to improve community health for everyone, and also provides resources (e.g., Webinar on Safe Routes for Older Adults) to promote those efforts. Two Canadian organizations, Sport for Life Society (https://sportforlife.ca) and Physical Literacy for Life (https://physicalliteracy.ca) have teamed up to provide resources for ensuring inclusivity (Physical Literacy Inclusion, https://physicalliteracy.ca/inclusion/) in physically active programs, and the Library for All (https://programminglibrarian.org/programs/library-all) in Golden, Colorado, offers tips for inclusive programming as well. For additional ideas and resources, and/or to share your projects and successes, please visit Let's Move in Libraries at https://letsmovelibraries.org/.

CHAPTER 6

Reference

Trares, R. (2020, September 27). "Fitness Program Encourages People to Get Active This Fall." *Daily Journal*. Accessed October 8, 2020. http://www.dailyjournal.net/2020/09/28/fitness_program_encourages_people_to_get_active_this_fall/

Implementing Opportunities

Sometimes the data may seem to point to a lack of interest in a topic, activity, or program, but it's important to keep in mind that there may be extenuating circumstances. For example, your event may have experienced extremely low attendance rates because the scheduling conflicted with the local dance studio's recital, or inclement weather, or the first sunny day in weeks. Thus, just because attendance may have not been what you expected or anticipated, this doesn't necessarily mean there wasn't interest in the program or that you should shelve a certain approach, idea, or activity permanently.

Query your "regulars," those patrons whom you might have expected to attend but didn't show up. If issues such as weather or competing events seem to be a factor, keep track of weather and weather-related issues and other local opportunities that were offered on the same days as your programs to determine if there are patterns emerging.

Some public library directors report success in gathering data by reaching out directly to community members through events such as focus groups at local venues such as restaurants. This enables a more candid discussion and helps to reach nonusers. To be truly effective in this type of data collection, consider hosting focus groups in a wide range of community gathering places, if possible. This could include local shops, fitness centers, food banks, shelters, salons, barber shops, clubs, service organizations, and places of worship.

RECAP

Many library services and activities have built-in data collection and feedback loops, and as program organizers and hosts, we are constantly integrating data to inform and improve our approaches. Once you have satisfied your constituents, in the final analysis, the data you collect and use will be only as valuable as the improvements you make with it.

REFERENCES

Datta, L-E. (1982). "A Tale of Two Studies: The Westinghouse-Ohio Evaluation of Project Head Start and the Consortium for Longitudinal Studies Report." *Studies in Educational Evaluation, 8*(3), 271–80. https://doi.org/10.1016/0191-491X(82)90031-1.

Westinghouse Learning Corporation. (1969). *The Impact of Head Start: An Evaluation of the Effects of Head Start on Children's Cognitive and Affective Development*. Athens: Ohio University Press/New York, NY: Westinghouse.

Yost, M. (2020, June 3). "19 Definitions of Success You Should Never Ignore." *Lifehack*. Accessed October 11, 2020. https://www.lifehack.org/articles/communication/the-new-definitions-success.html

7

THE LIFE CYCLE OF LIBRARY PROGRAMMING

The goal of this final chapter is to combine the concepts presented in earlier chapters and to consider the life cycle of library programs. In order to achieve this, we'll move through a template that describes how a library program or event moves through the logical stages from

idea → planning → promoting → hosting → evaluating → reporting → lessons learned → tweaking → offer again, offer differently, or discontinue.

The chapter concludes with a discussion of libraries and programs with regard to environmental sustainability, pointing to additional resources for sustainability considerations and for program and event support in general.

MODEL PROGRAM: LEARNING AND LEAPING WITH THE LIBRARY

Idea Generation

When it comes to library programs, ideas for activities are usually generated and considered somewhat automatically within the larger organizational framework. Hence, they're likely already inherently tied to an overarching organizational goal (e.g., increasing library visibility and patronage) or the library's larger mission (e.g., increased community access to educational and recreational opportunities). In the case of an earlier example, the teen juggling workshop discussed in chapter 4, the idea was borne out of a need to engage a segment of

CHAPTER 7

the library's community that was somewhat underserved and underrepresented. Ideas might also be proposed that extend current goals or approach fulfilling the library's mission in a novel way. Thus, it's generally a very welcome sound to a program director's ears when a staff member says, "I have an idea for a program."

Perhaps after completing a community assessment, you've learned there are a number of prevalent preventable health conditions in all demographic ranges in your area, so your team has decided that a primary goal for the library's upcoming five-year plan should be to provide an array of opportunities that support engagement in physical activities. This could dovetail nicely with the goal of bringing in a range of age groups and extending the library's reach into the greater community.

Planning

Let's assume that the broad goal—*The library will support community health and well-being by providing opportunities for engaging in physical activity for all age groups*—has been established and agreed upon. The next phase in the process involves creating and defining more specific goals and objectives. These may differ slightly for each demographic group, and each program will also have individual objectives. To move the plan forward, we'll return to our ABCD method of setting objectives for the overall program initiative and for individual programs. For example, for the broad goal to support activities that encourage a more active community, the following might apply:

- A = Audience: Who is the target audience?
    - Overall community
        - This will be split into subgroups by age (e.g., toddlers and preschoolers, elementary, middle, and high-schoolers, young adults, middle-aged, seniors) for convenience in program provision, though programs will be open to everyone.
- B = Behavior: What will be accomplished?
    - Increase in physical activity level
        - How will this be measured and/or observed (e.g., with pre- and post-surveys, provision of tracking devices, self-reports, observation, etc.)?
        - What behaviors will be seen (e.g., attendance at active programs, walking groups on local trails, story time groups at the local playground, etc.)?

- C = Condition: Under what circumstances will behavior occur?
  - Various intervals
    - By the end of one month, six months, one year
- D = Degree: To what extent will the behavior need to be performed?
  - For example, patrons will engage in at least one activity each month

For creating objectives for specific programs for each age demographic (such as a walking group for seniors or a juggling workshop for teens), the same approach applies, and the ABCD method can be used as a guide. Once goals and objectives are outlined, the next steps are to create a more detailed timeline and task list, and to identify milestones. As a starting point, team members can brainstorm and create a crude table, such as the one shown in table 7.1.

This exercise could provide a framework to address some of the preliminary considerations outlined in chapter 1, including the likely audience, potential collaborators, and a rudimentary timeline. Examination of how you will ensure accessibility and inclusivity overall and for each group should be addressed at this stage, too. Other aspects for contemplation in the planning phase include: What resources are needed? Are there qualified volunteers or staff members who can lead programs? Are there items in collection (e.g., books, videos, YouTube instructions, LibGuides, adaptive toys) that can be used in the program and/or for promotional displays? Are there other libraries that have had successful programs you can model?

Table 7.2 provides a preliminary framework that can be easily adapted for the next steps of outlining tasks and ensuring additional details are covered. Of course, each process will be characteristic of the individual organization, so these tables are provided as examples of ways to approach and are not meant to be exhaustive.

Promoting

Responsibility for promotion may be assigned to a public relations or communications department, or may fall upon the program librarian, manager, or director. No matter the size of the department or resources available, basic promotion tools include press releases (American Library Association, n.d.), the library's regular media tools, public service announcements, website, listservs, banners, and posters.

Table 7.1. Planning Considerations

Responsible Team Member	Audience	Initial Program Ideas	Potential Collaborators	Resources Needed	Timeline
Children's librarian	Toddlers Preschool School-age	Active story time; hiking group	Head Start; local preschools	None—books and adaptive tools are already available	Can implement immediately
YA librarian	Young adults	Juggling workshop; dance party	School librarian; PE teacher; local coaches	Instructor; videos; tennis balls; rice	Depending on instructor, rm. availability, w/in the month
Program librarian	Adults	Walking group; juggling team	Local hiking, birdwatching groups	Instructor; videos; tennis balls; rice	Depending on instructor, rm. availability, w/in the month
Program librarian Outreach librarian	Seniors	Gentle yoga; chair stretches	Arthritis Foundation; local healthcare	Instructor; training for staff	Depending on program, staff resources, rm. availability, w/in the month
Outreach librarian Program librarian	Homeless	Tai-chi or exercise on the front lawn	Local shelter; social service agencies	Instructor; training for staff, depending on location, security (e.g., partitioning off outdoor space)	Depending on program, staff resources, w/in the month
Program librarian Outreach librarian	Working parents	Yoga classes; juggling team	Local fitness outlets	Instructor; offer babysitting	Can implement immediately
Program librarian Outreach librarian	Immigrants, accounting for cultural considerations	Walking partners	Local organizations; Parks & Rec. Department	Offer ESL tutoring while taking a walk; audiobooks for listening to while exercising	Can implement immediately
Program librarian Outreach librarian	Other specific demographic subsets of your community	Tailored for audience	Parks & Rec. Department	Depends on program	Depends on program

Table 7.2. Preliminary Framework

Tasks	Who's responsible	Timing	Notes	Contingencies
Identify, invite presenter	Program librarian	Weeks-months ahead of event	Consider options for inclusivity and accessibility	Virtual options, e.g., Zoom, Skype
Coordinate schedule	Admin. support staff; Program librarian	Weeks-months ahead of event	Ensure extra staff are on hand if needed	For outdoor, is a rain date necessary?
Location arrangements (e.g., reserving space)	Admin. support staff	Weeks-months ahead of event	Is space accessible and inviting	Virtual options
Promotion activities	Admin. support staff; Program librarian	Weeks-months ahead of event	Responsibility depends on program, etc.	Virtual options
Host program: Welcome presenter, attendees; distribute evaluation materials (if needed); monitor room, activities	Program librarian; Admin. support staff	Day of event If pre-test occurs prior to day event is held, determine timing		Identify alternative rooms, venues in case of hiccups
Thank-you notes to speaker(s)	Program librarian; Admin. support staff	Immediately following program or event	Depending on event, director may also be responsible	E-mail can be used for expediency
Record and tabulate data: attendance, surveys, observations	Program librarian; Support staff; Administration	As soon as possible post-event		Get enthused student intern to do follow-up assessment
Reflect on data	Program librarian; Library team members	As soon as possible post-event; ideally within 1–3 months	Review program data on a regular basis to spot trends, etc.	Get student intern or outsider to assess
Report data	Program librarian; Administration	As required or established—e.g., monthly newsletters, annual report	Consider multiple venues	

CHAPTER 7

For the physical activity promotion programs, promotion could start by creating a community buzz. For example, questions such as these could be posted around town and on social media:

- What are the four types of exercise that can improve your health and physical ability?
  - Answer: endurance, strength, balance, and flexibility (National Institute on Aging, n.d.).
  - The National Institute on Aging website also provides further information, explanation, safety tips, and examples, all of which could be used for program ideas on each of the four types of exercise.
- Did you know if you exercise with a partner or in a group, you're more likely to commit time to it?
  - Yes, research demonstrates a plethora of benefits.
    - According to one study, 95 percent of participants who started a weight-loss program with their friends finished it, compared to 76 percent of those who did it on their own (Wing & Jeffery, 1999).
    - Other studies show that working out with someone increases the amount of time spent exercising (Irwin et al., 2012).
- Did you know that juggling helps brain development?
  - Yes, among many benefits for all age groups, juggling enhances brain connectivity (Scholz et al., 2009).
- Did you know that when parents are physically active, their children will be more likely to follow?
  - Yes, children of active mothers were found to be 2 times more likely to be active than those of inactive mothers.
  - Children of active parents were 5.8 times more likely to be active than those of inactive parents (Moore, 1991).

These questions are to get the ball rolling; such an approach could be easily adapted for specific community interests and issues, include prizes, and so on. The answers to questions could be posted at the library entrance and on the library's website and social media, with details on programs.

In some cases, ready-made resources are available for promotional activities, such as the Event Toolkit for Preservation Week from the ALA's Association for Library Collections and Technical Services, which provides logos, bookmarks, fliers, and all types of tools. The toolkit is available at http://www.ala.org/alcts/preservationweek/tools.

HOSTING

The actual hosting details of individual programs (i.e., where, when, who, what activities, what resources are needed for activities) will have been determined during the planning phase. Thus, logistics on the actual program day will be prescribed by what has already been planned. For instance, if the program is a panel discussion by local healthcare experts on the benefits of physical activity, the venue will likely be the library's community room, and the responsibility of room setup and cleanup will have been predetermined. The program librarian will welcome everyone, introduce the panel, and attend to any issues that arise.

Attendance data should be collected during this time and can include gate counts, how many seats are filled (or not), and registration (if this was required). Sign-in sheets with a column for age and zip code can help collect data on where folks came from and what age segment was in attendance. If there's an evaluation component, this should be explained and/or distributed as well. Contingency plans should also be in place for emergencies, such as power outages, weather events, and illness.

Evaluation

How will we know we're successful? Well-formed, concrete goals and objectives with predetermined targets for data collection and a built-in evaluation plan will help to determine and describe levels of program success. If an evaluation component hasn't been built in or planned, a short sample survey could be provided to participants that captures their engagement with minimal effort. The survey could be distributed at the conclusion of the program and include questions such as "What did you like best/least about the program?" "What are two things you will take away from the program?" and "Do you have suggestions for other programs?"

In the case of the physical activity campaign, each individual program initiative will collect specific program data (e.g., how many families engaged in active story time offerings, how many seniors joined the walking group, how many teens attended the juggling workshop and returned for follow-up activities, etc.) and data from individuals on their experience. Data from all of the programs and offerings can then be combined to give a big-picture account throughout the course of the campaign. For example, the library could post results like, "Together, we've walked 600 miles in the past month"; "In the past year, 432

CHAPTER 7

community members attended fitness programs at the library"; and "Participants rated the Riverwalk Trail as the best place to walk in our community."

Reporting

Depending on the library's routine, program data will be shared through various internal and external mechanisms. Within the organization, sharing might be informal, such as reporting and comparing program results at regular staff meetings or through shared memos and the like. External reporting will likely compile a variety of data (e.g., attendance numbers, participants' reactions, program description) to give a textured description of program results. These reports are then shared with library users, the greater community, funders, and oversight committees through mechanisms such as the library's website, newsletter, social media, annual reports, and so on. In the example of the physical activity campaign, results could be shared with the local health department and social service agencies to extend partnerships and incite collaborative activities.

Lessons Learned

After the program has occurred, it is important to reflect upon what was learned. These could be simple lessons, such as the capacity of the community room when it comes to teens' juggling space or the skill and comfort level of staff when it comes to leading exercise routines. If there isn't already a mechanism in place for sharing or recording what was learned through the experience, create one. This could be as simple as the program coordinator keeping a log of "what I would do differently next time." Regular review and application of these lessons will engender stronger programming in the future.

Tweaking

Lessons learned naturally leads to the tweaking stage and the decision whether to continue with a program as is, to change and offer it again, or to abandon the idea altogether. A lesson might be as simple as observing that for a fitness session more instructors are needed for one-to-one interaction for participants, or that more staff are needed to participate in walking groups because the attendance is so high. To make changes, it's necessary to record and keep track of what you've learned. In this way, you can share with your colleagues, and apply changes as needed.

Future Plans

Once the program has been offered, the data you've collected should point to whether a program is successful and whether it should be continued and/or adapted. Enthusiastic interest in a program might in itself signify how to extend efforts. For instance, if juggling workshops are successful and a town juggling craze takes over, the library might start a traveling juggling troupe or hire an instructor who can engage participants at a higher skill level. Future plans might also entail working with neighboring libraries to assess interest and compare results across communities.

In the next section, we will shift gears to address the role libraries play in environmental sustainability and how sustainable thinking can be applied to library programs.

ENVIRONMENTAL SUSTAINABILITY CONSIDERATIONS

While political issues come and go, there may be no issue that will more certainly be a priority for library users over the next half century than stopping the degradation of our global environment. Environmental sustainability requires global commitment, one in which libraries can be active participants.

Sustainability has been defined as "meeting the needs of present generations without compromising the ability of future generations to meet their needs" (United Nations, 1987). This definition allows for a broad interpretation of ways organizations can support sustainability. Many libraries have stepped up to the plate with new construction often tied to Leadership in Energy and Environmental Design (LEED) certification and organization-wide initiatives around sustainability considerations. However, as Aulisio (2013) aptly points out, "green" libraries are about more than architecture; the library's mission, rather than inherent and inherited architecture, is the true driving force in how libraries operate with regard to promoting sustainability.

Given that most libraries are in the business of sharing resources, they provide services and operate in contexts that innately promote sustainable use of resources. An obvious way in which libraries seamlessly support sustainability is through lending—providing access not only to books but to all sorts and types of items, which helps minimize wide-scale consumerism. From cake pans to tools to bikes to interview apparel, folks who need to use an item for a limited number of times, want to try something out without the financial commitment, or might not otherwise have the opportunity to use such an item can find it at

CHAPTER 7

their library. Public access to computers, printers, scanners, and the like is still important to a large segment of the population. More and more, makerspaces within libraries offer access to equipment such as sewing machines, 3D printers, laser cutters, photography studios, and other resources that community members might not otherwise have the opportunity to use.

Providing space for meetings, individual work, and projects is another way in which libraries support sustainability, through maximizing a shared communal resource. Individual workspaces are often available for all community members, such as students as well as self-employed, retired, and unemployed people. Group spaces are also available for use at most libraries and are offered for free or for a nominal charge. A variety of activities are supported in this way, such as meeting space for the entire community, including local organizations and clubs. Beyond these obvious examples, in this day and age, every activity the library organization engages in should be considered and assessed through a lens of "sustainable thinking," which is also the title of a valuable resource for guiding libraries at this "all-hands-on-deck moment in history" (Aldrich, 2018, p. 25).

What Does Sustainability Mean for Programs and Events?

As libraries address sustainability concerns in a variety of ways, some are including program provision in their efforts. For example, the Kingston Library in Kingston, New York, made a pledge in 2010 in which it supported the town's 2009 Climate Smart, Green Jobs pledge (Kingston Library, 2010). The library's trustees resolved to reduce greenhouse gas emissions and take actions to adapt in our changing climate. In terms of library programs specifically, the pledge includes the following actions:

1. Including climate change actions in programs to engage the community
2. Providing opportunities to support mitigation and adaptation efforts through provision of library materials that inform on climate change, climate protection, sustainability, and environmental services
3. Leading by example through reduced energy consumption, and transparent reporting on greenhouse gas emission targets to the library community
4. Demonstrating benefits of water conservation, recycling, and renewable energy products by communicating progress on goals to the library community

5. Encouraging walking, bicycling, carpooling, and public transportation for staff and patrons, as ways to reduce their carbon footprint
6. Working with the community and neighboring libraries to adapt actions and boost positive results

On another note, the Kingston Library also provides a great model for sharing data with the community. In October 2020, upon visiting the library website, the viewer is greeted with a red banner at the top of the page in all capital letters, stating: "KINGSTON LIBRARY DISTRICT'S 2021 TAX LEVY OF $916,455 WAS APPROVED BY A VOTE OF 129 YES TO 12 NO ... THANK YOU TO CITY OF KINGSTON VOTERS FOR YOUR CONTINUING SUPPORT!" What an effective way to share the library's gratitude and acknowledgment of the community's appreciation of the library!

Engaging in sustainable efforts can also mean seemingly small efforts, like using LED light bulbs, programmable thermostats, reusable dishes, cups, name tags, and the like, as well as water pitchers for guest speakers instead of bottled water.

CONSIDERING THE TRUE COSTS OF BOTTLED WATER

Worldwide consumption of bottled water is up to 1.5 billion plastic bottles daily. That's equivalent to about 1 million plastic bottles per minute (Laville & Taylor, 2017). In the United States, 33 billion liters of bottled water are consumed per year, even though most people who buy bottled water have access to water for free (or with minimal fees—on average, tap water is less than a penny per gallon). Nonetheless, consumption of bottled water is higher than that of beer and milk (Gleick & Cooley, 2009).

Production of bottled water requires up to two thousand times the energy needed to provide tap water; the manufacturing of an average plastic water bottle requires about 1.85 gallons of water to produce (Merchant, 2018). Not only do these plastic bottles take large amounts of energy to make, they further contribute to carbon emissions (from shipping), and they're difficult to get rid of—our landfills and waterways are becoming heaps of plastic. Eight million tons of plastic lands in our oceans every year (International Union for Conservation of Nature, 2018).

Cutting back on bottled water consumption could have profound positive environmental benefits by helping to reduce carbon emissions, curbing extravagant water use, and reducing garbage production, with less plastic ending up in our oceans and landfills.

CHAPTER 7

Given that bottled water is so ecologically unsustainable and the topic is relatively apolitical, an educational program and/or display on the benefits of reducing bottled water consumption could be a ready-made way to initiate a community conversation about sustainability. Reusable water bottles printed with the library's logo and tips for reducing your carbon footprint could be raffled off or given out to program attendees.

REFERENCES

Gleick, P. H., & Cooley, H. S. (2009). "Energy Implications of Bottled Water." *Environmental Research Letters 4*. Accessed October 14, 2020. https://phys.org/news/2009-03-energy-bottle.html#:~:text=Combining%20all%20the%20energy%20input,bottle%20is%20about%200.5%20liters)

International Union for Conservation of Nature. (2018). Issues Brief: Marine Plastic. Accessed October 9, 2020. https://www.iucn.org/resources/issues-briefs/marine-plastics

Laville, S., & Taylor, M. (2017, June 28). "A Million Bottles a Minute: World's Plastic Binge 'as Dangerous as Climate Change.'" *Guardian*. Accessed October 9, 2020. https://www.theguardian.com/environment/2017/jun/28/a-million-a-minute-worlds-plastic-bottle-binge-as-dangerous-as-climate-change

Merchant, B. (2018, October 11). "How Many Gallons of Water Does It Take to Make . . ." *Treehugger*. Accessed October 14, 2020. https://www.treehugger.com/how-many-gallons-of-water-does-it-take-to-make-4858491

If you use print surveys, recycle them, and in general, make all types of recycling easy for patrons and staff. If possible, install hand dryers in the public restrooms, reducing paper waste. Use the space above the hand dryer to update patrons on upcoming programs or news items—you have a captive audience for thirty seconds. Sustainability also means big efforts like pivoting and repurposing, such as during the COVID-19 pandemic, when library makerspaces became mask-making providers and supplied a needed resource throughout the community.

COVID-19 has changed and is changing our approaches to everything we do, personally and professionally. Professional conferences have shifted to virtual formats, so the need to travel to national and international venues has plummeted. As we move forward in our new ways of doing things, careful consideration should be taken. For instance, perhaps our habits of expending carbon dioxide to meet in person can be amended; it may make sense to change to biannual in-person conferences, with every other year taking place virtually.

Closing Thoughts

We know on a visceral level that libraries have the capacity to change communities and to do great things. We know that they are tied to higher property values; when their budgets are voted on, they are approved by the public more often than school budgets are. Libraries are widely trusted. Because people are so fond and supportive of libraries and so appreciative of library programs, we are generally not expected to justify our choices or to prove the worth of our programs. This is of some concern, for two reasons. First, the data and evaluations that show impact arise from the same processes that tell us how we can do a better job. And second, whether we want to or not, libraries are being drawn into more and more complicated issues at a faster and faster rate—and this is a great thing because it increases libraries' social value. Being expected to facilitate people getting insurance via the Affordable Care Act, teaching computer literacy, keeping programs going by Zoom during COVID-19, and supporting remote teaching are difficult and complicated tasks. But they are profound and socially constructive tasks. Librarians, by their nature, cannot help but address the issues in their communities, and as these issues become more and more challenging, our ability to critically assess what we are doing and how to do it better will only become more central to our missions. We need library programs like never before. But we also need to be systematic, professional, and self-critical like never before, if we are to keep our position as one of the most trusted institutions in our communities.

RECAP

Recognizing that each initiative, program, and library setting will be unique, this chapter summarized the process of and considerations for program planning and provided templates for moving from planning to promoting to hosting and evaluation of program performance. As we move through the decades to come, environmental and global sustainability efforts will likely be in the forefront of everything we do, and so the volume ends with an exhortation to consider not only the impact of programs, but the impact of the library as well.

REFERENCES

Aldrich, R. S. (2018). *Sustainable Thinking*. Chicago, IL: American Library Association.

CHAPTER 7

American Library Association (n.d.). "Tips for Writing Press Releases." Preservation Week. http://www.ala.org/alcts/preservationweek/plan/pressrelease

Aulisio, G. J. (2013). "Green Libraries Are More Than Just Buildings." *Electronic Green Journal, 1*(35), 1–8.

Irwin, B. C., Schorniaenchi, J., Kerr, N. L., et al. (2012). "Aerobic Exercise Is Promoted When Individual Performance Affects the Group: A Test of the Kohler Motivation Gain Effect." *Annals of Behavioral Medicine, 44*, 151–59.

Kingston Library. (2010, September 16). *Climate Smart Community Library Pledge*. Accessed October 19, 2020. https://www.kingstonlibrary.org/wp-content/uploads/2019/12/kl_climate_smart_pledge.pdf

Moore, L. L., Lombardi, D. A., White, M. J., Campbell, J. L., Oliveria, S. A., & Ellison, R. C. (1991). "Influence of Parents' Physical Activity Levels on Activity Levels of Young Children." *Journal of Pediatrics, 118*(2), 215–19. PMID: 1993947.

National Institute on Aging. (n.d.). "Four Types of Exercise Can Improve Your Health and Physical Ability." Accessed December 5, 2020. https://www.nia.nih.gov/health/four-types-exercise-can-improve-your-health-and-physical-ability

Scholz, J., et al. (2009). "Training Induces Changes in White-Matter Architecture." *Nature Neuroscience, 12*(11), 1370–71.

United Nations. (1987). *Report of the World Commission on Environment and Development: Our Common Future*. Accessed December 5, 2020. http://www.un-documents.net/wced-ocf.htm

Wing, R. R., & Jeffery, R. W. (1999). "Benefits of Recruiting Participants with Friends and Increasing Social Support for Weight Loss and Maintenance." *Journal of Consulting and Clinical Psychology, 67*(1), 132–38. PMID: 10028217.

RESOURCES

GENERAL RESOURCES

Banks, C. S., & Mediavilla, C. (2019). *Libraries and Gardens: Growing Together.* Chicago, IL: American Library Association.
Dodge, H. (2020). *Gather 'Round the Table: Food Literacy Programs, Resources, and Ideas for Libraries.* Chicago, IL: American Library Association.
Dudley, M. (ed.). (2013). *Public Libraries and Resilient Cities.* Chicago, IL: American Library Association.
Flaherty, M. G. (2018). *Promoting Individual and Community Health at the Library.* Chicago, IL: American Library Association.
Houde, L. (2018). *Serving LGBTQ Teens: A Practical Guide for Librarians.* Lanham, MD: Rowman & Littlefield.
Jones, S. D., & Murphy, B. (2020). *Diversity in Libraries: A Call to Action and Strategies for Success.* Lanham, MD: Rowman & Littlefield.
Marrall, R. (2020). *Developing a Library Accessibility Plan: A Practical Guide for Librarians.* Lanham, MD: Rowman & Littlefield.

FURTHER PROGRAMMING RESOURCES

Alessio, A. J., Lamantia, K., & Vinci, E. (2019). *50+ Programs for Tweens, Teens, Adults, and Families: 12 Months of Ideas.* Chicago, IL: American Library Association.
Batykefer, E., & Damon-Moore, L. (2019). *Incubating Creativity at Your Library: A Sourcebook for Connecting with Communities.* Chicago, IL: American Library Association.

RESOURCES

Bruno, T. (2018). *Gaming Programs for All Ages at the Library: A Practical Guide for Librarians*. Lanham, MD: Rowman & Littlefield.

Campana, K., & Mill, J. E. (eds.). (2019). *Create, Innovate, and Serve: A Radical Approach to Children's and Youth Programming*. Chicago, IL: American Library Association.

Carson, J. (2019). *Yoga and Meditation at the Library: A Practical Guide for Librarians*. Lanham, MD: Rowman & Littlefield.

Demeter, M., & Holmes, H. K. (2018). *Library Programming Made Easy: A Practical Guide for Librarians*. Lanham, MD: Rowman & Littlefield.

Denzer, J., & Ginsberg, S. (2020). *Terrific Makerspace Projects: A Practical Guide for Librarians*. Lanham, MD: Rowman & Littlefield.

Fournier, M. D., & Ostman, S. (eds.). (2020). *Ask, Listen, Empower: Grounding Your Library Work in Community Engagement*. Chicago, IL: American Library Association.

Hanick, R., Bateman, M., & Burek Pierce, J. (2019). *Mapping the Imaginary: Supporting Creative Writers through Programming, Prompts, and Research*. Chicago, IL: American Library Association.

Hughes, K., & Santoro, J. (eds.). (2020). *The 24/7 Library: Ideas for Serving Your Community Anytime, Anywhere*. Chicago, IL: American Library Association.

Jewell, A. (2019). *Move, Play, Learn: Interactive Storytimes with Music, Movement, and More*. Chicago, IL: American Library Association.

Kirker, C. M. (2018). *25 Projects for Art Explorers*. Chicago, IL: American Library Association.

Kirker, C. M. (2019). *25 Projects for Global Explorers*. Chicago, IL: American Library Association.

Kirker, C. M. (2020). *25 Projects for Eco Explorers*. Chicago, IL: American Library Association.

Kroski, E. (ed.). (2017). *The Makerspace Librarian's Sourcebook*. Chicago, IL: American Library Association.

Kroski, E. (ed.). (2019). *Escape Rooms and Other Immersive Experiences in the Library*. Chicago, IL: American Library Association.

Kroski, E. (ed.). (2019). *53 Ready-to-Use Kawaii Craft Projects*. Chicago, IL: American Library Association.

Kroski, E. (ed.). (2019). *60 Ready-to-Use Coding Projects*. Chicago, IL: American Library Association.

Lenstra, N. (2020). *Healthy Living at the Library: Programs for All Ages*. Santa Barbara, CA: Libraries Unlimited.

Ludt, R. (2020). *Think Big! A Resource Manual for Teen Library Programs That Attract Large Audiences*. Lanham, MD: Rowman & Littlefield.

McChesney, E., & Nicholas, B. (2020). *Pairing STEAM with Stories: 46 Hands-On Activities for Children*. Chicago, IL: American Library Association.

RESOURCES

Ostman, S., & Saba, S. (2019). *Book Club Reboot: 71 Creative Twists*. Chicago, IL: American Library Association.

Pard, C. (2018). *STEM Programming for All Ages: A Practical Guide for Librarians*. Lanham, MD: Rowman & Littlefield.

Pard, C. (2020). *Anime Clubs for Public Libraries*. Lanham, MD: Rowman & Littlefield.

Price, C. (2020). *209 Big Programming Ideas for Small Budgets*. Chicago, IL: American Library Association.

Tuccillo, D. P. (2020). *Totally Tweens and Teens: Youth-Created and Youth-Led Library Programs*. Lanham, MD: Rowman & Littlefield.

Walter, V. A. (2020). *Young Activists and the Public Library: Facilitating Democracy*. Chicago, IL: American Library Association.

INDEX

absentee voter registration, 54–58
asynchronous workshop, 23
audience, 4

Bloom, Suzanne, 93–94
Bowles, Vickery, 88–90
Brody, Erica, 47–49

collaboration, 5, 6, 72, 75, 104, 116
community assessment, 4, 8
community engagement, 4
county health rankings, 4

data collection, 68, 76–78
data sources, 75
disability, 9

focus groups, 74, 106
Foundations, 36
Friends groups, 35

gamification, 49
Gibson, Amelia, 7–14
goals, 5, 66, 80, 98
government funding agencies, 37

inclusion, 7–14, 105
interviews, 74, 76

Johnson, Taylor, 58–62

Ledbetter, Leila, 51–53
Lenstra, Noah, 49–51, 124

makerspace, 21–23
marketing strategies, 44
Melo, Maggie, 21–23
Miller, David, 99–101
mission, 2

Neuroth, Lydia, 17–21

objectives, 5, 66, 67, 80, 110–11
observation, 74, 77
outcome measures, 69

program topics, 15, 16
Project Outcome, 78

qualitative research methods, 73, 74
quantitative research methods, 73, 74
questionnaires, 74, 78

INDEX

ready-made themes, 14–16
records review, 74
Reece, Gwendolyn, 54–58
remote workshop, 22
research methods, 73
Robert Wood Johnson Foundation, 4

sample programs, 17–23, 32–35, 47–62, 70–72, 79, 99–101, 104–106
service organizations, 38
SMART objectives, 67

stakeholders, 86
surveys, 74, 78, 101–102
sustainability, 117–120
synchronous workshop, 23

therapy dogs, 51–53
triangulation, 75–76

universal design, 12–13
universities and colleges, 38

zine-making, 17–21

ABOUT THE AUTHOR

Mary Grace Flaherty is an associate professor in the School of Information and Library Science at the University of North Carolina at Chapel Hill. She received her PhD from Syracuse University, where she was an IMLS Fellow. Mary Grace has her MLS from the University of Maryland and an MS in Applied Behavioral Science from Johns Hopkins University. Before turning to teaching and engaging with the next generation of librarians, Mary Grace worked in a variety of library settings, including academic, health research, public, and special.

www.ingramcontent.com/pod-product-compliance
Lightning Source LLC
Chambersburg PA
CBHW022015300426
44117CB00005B/205